25th Anniversary *of* Bangladesh
In Trafalgar Square, London, UK

MAYAR AKASH

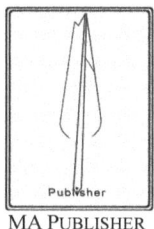

MA PUBLISHER

Mayar Akash

The right of Mayar Akash to be identified as the author of this work has been asserted in accordance with sections 77 and 78 of the Copyright Design and Patent Act 1988.

Thank you to Ansar Ahmed Ullah for supplying me the date, 14th April 1996.

Copyright © Mayar Akash 2021

Published by MA Publishing (Penzance)
Published June 2021
ISBN-13: 978-1-910499-72-6

All rights reserved. No part of this publication may be reproduced, stored in a retrieval system, or transmitted, in any form or by any means, electronic, mechanical, photocopying, recording, public performances or otherwise, without prior written permission of the copyright holder, except for brief quotations embodied in critical articles or reviews.

Cover designed by Mayar Akash
Typeset in Times New Roman
All photos belong to Mayar Akash

Paper printed on is FSC Certified, lead free, acid free, buffered paper made from wood-based pulp. Our paper meets the ISO 9706 standard for permanent paper. As such, paper will last several hundred years when stored.

Introduction

2021 is the 50th year of Bangladesh and as such the Bangladeshi community in UK are celebrating the 50th anniversary through various projects. The celebrations and festivities are subdued because of the Covid 19 pandemic and the lockdown restrictions; but nevertheless various events have taken place.

25 years ago, 14th of April 1996, as a younger man I was in Trafalgar Square, London, taking photos of the event that took place, under the Nelson's column and the Gallery. There I was impressionable and a photography enthusiast attending and taking photos.

This event was before the digital photography, using 35mm film negatives. While I wasn't in the politics but as a photojournalist, it was a setting to capture memorable shots and at the time – the thoughts was maybe one day I'll do something with them.

We know that so much has changed and also so many people in the photos are no longer with us. Though they are not my relations I look at the photos memorably; as we once shared the same space in our lives; where they crossed paths.

So, as they will live in my memories, I want to share them with those who, it will mean something to them.

The photos in the book are not the first generations prints from the negatives but scans from the first prints. Over time the images have taken on their tinges. After 25 years, all I can say is that I don't know where the negatives have gone but I'm glad that I had the photos scanned some while back.

So I hope you will enjoy the pictures and also how I chose to capture the images.

Joy Bangla

Joy Bangla!
Our sonar Bangladesh
Victorious souls
That ripples the nation

Joy Bangla!
Our land of joy and laughter
Home of our ancestors.

Joy Bangla!
Our mother land
Our fuel for hunger.

Joy Bangla!
Our sonar Bangla
Enriched with finest beauty.

A world of its own to be discovered.

The wisdom which lies untouched
Yet to be reborn
Yet to gain
And yet it shall rise again.

Trafalgar Square, London, UK, 14th April 1996

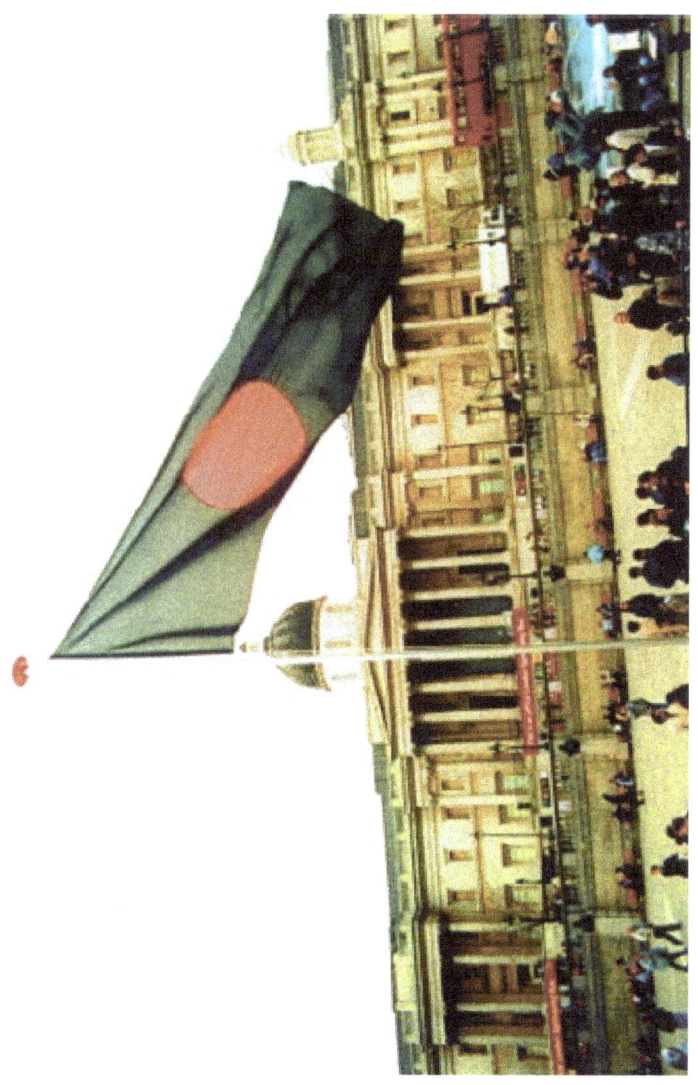

Lion & the Flag

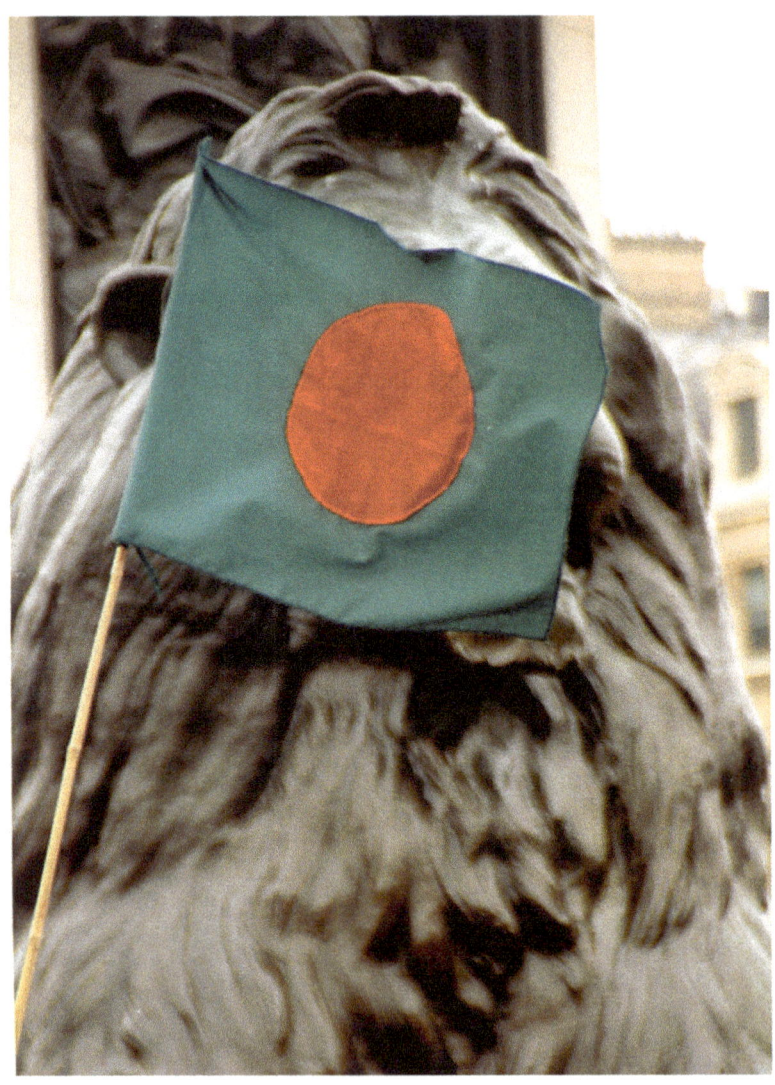

Under Nelson

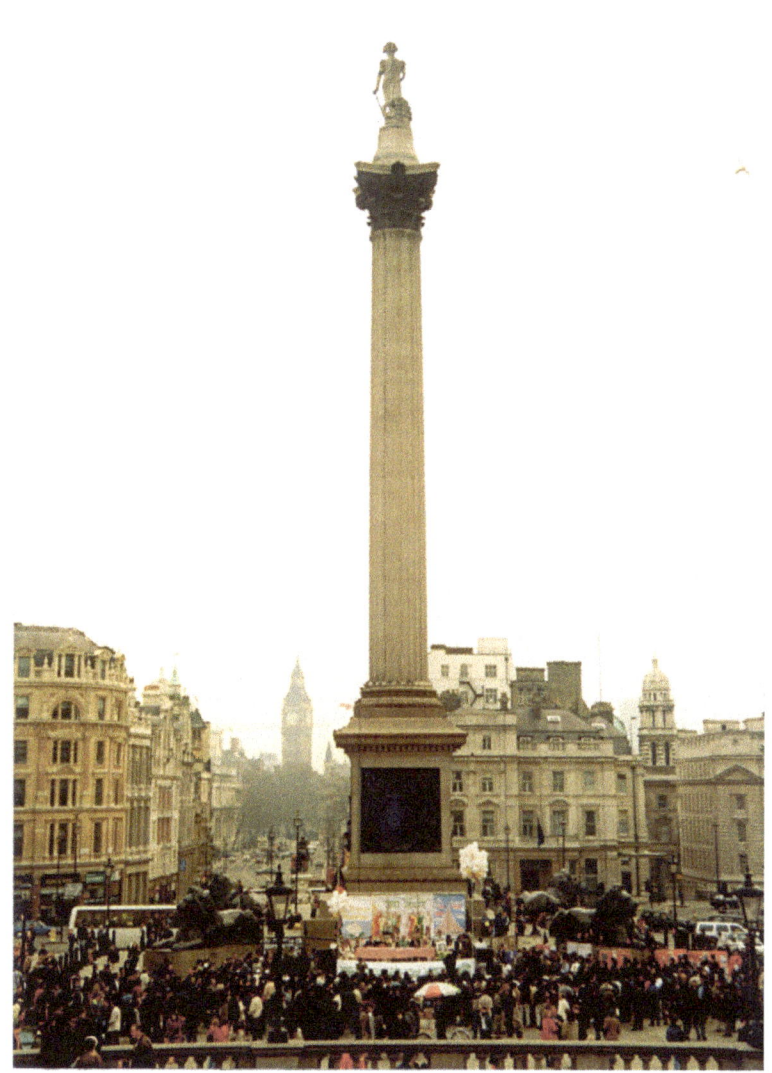

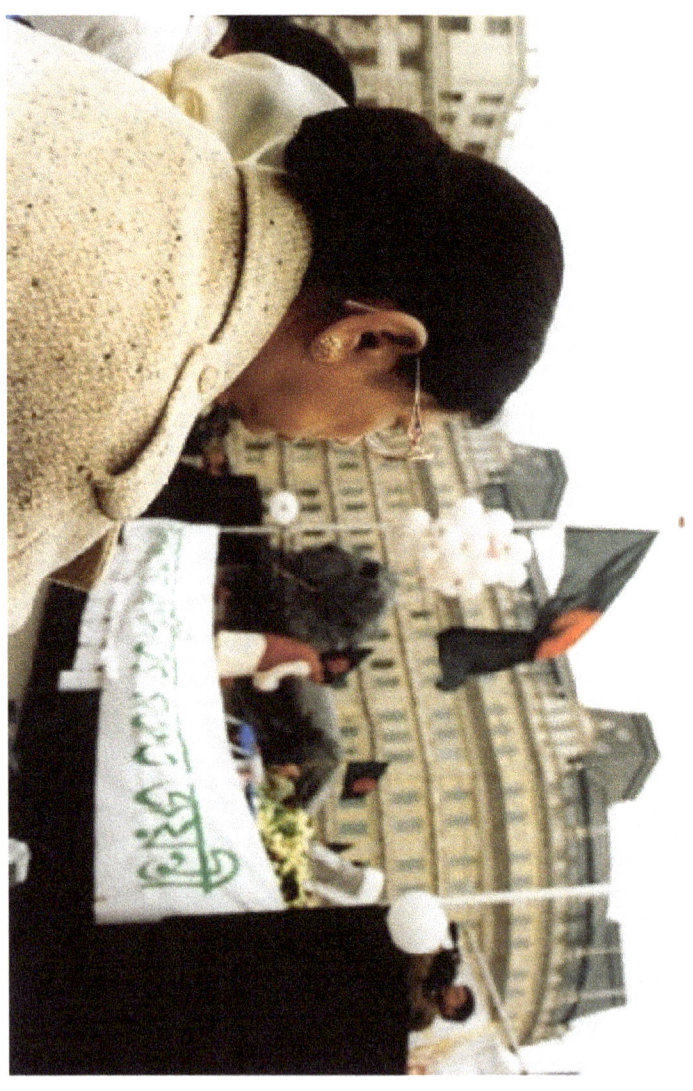

25th Anniversary of Bangladesh in Trafalgar Squares

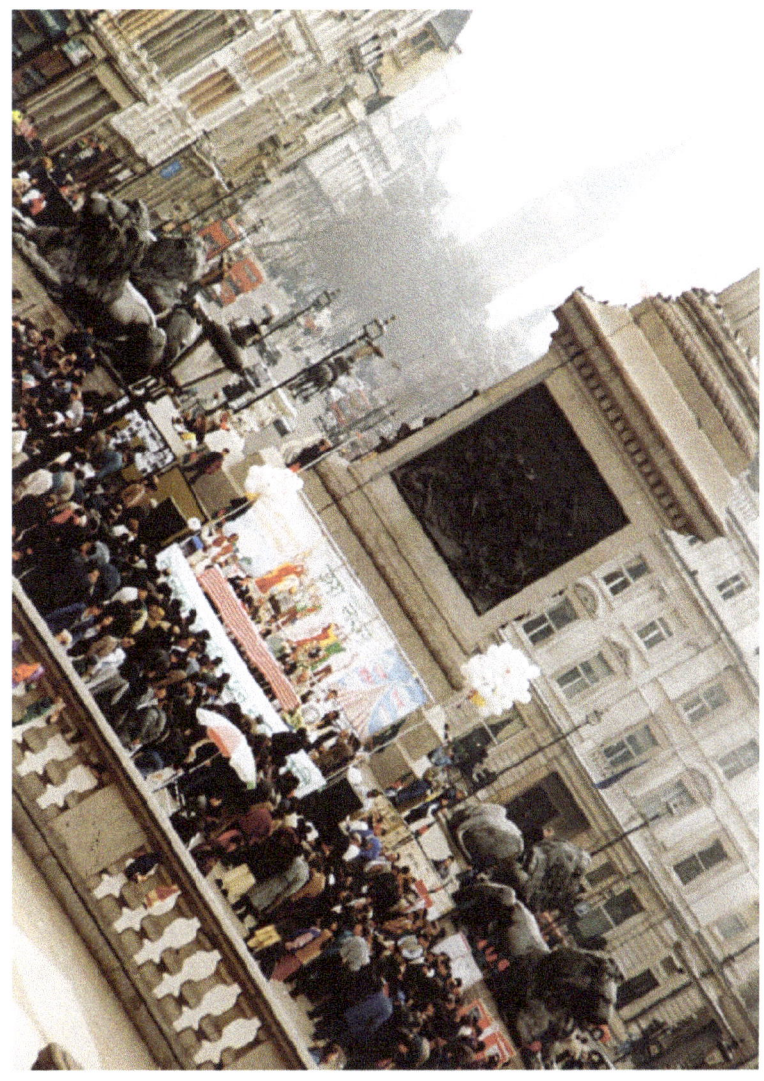

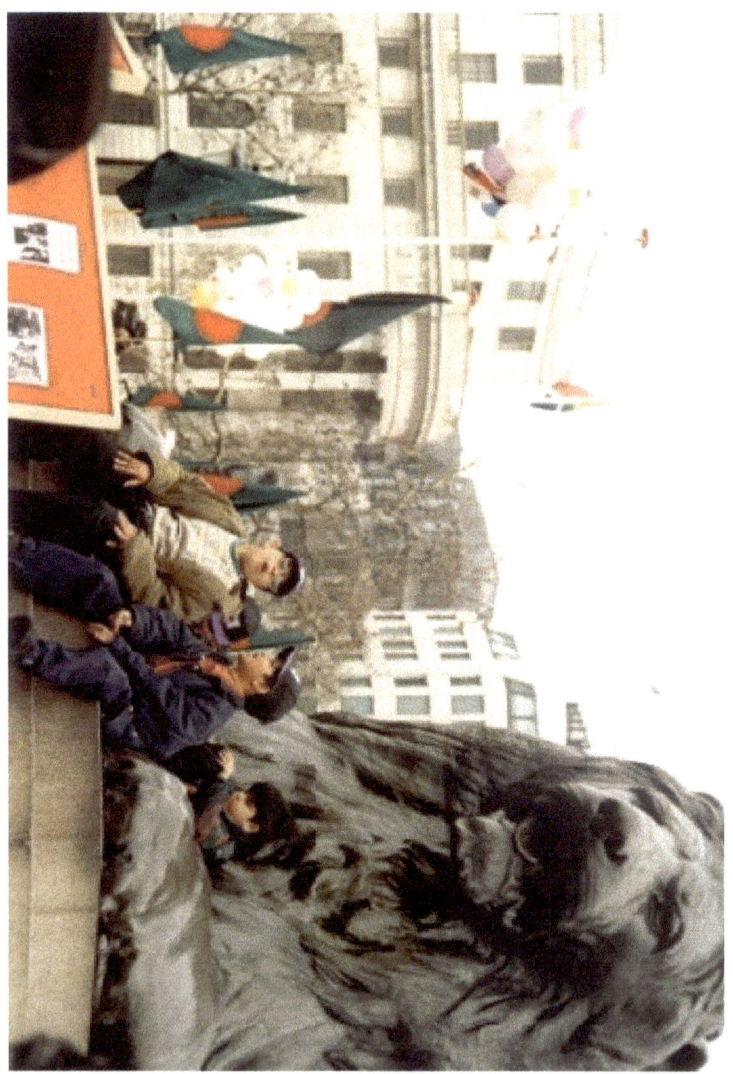

25th Anniversary of Bangladesh in Trafalgar Squares

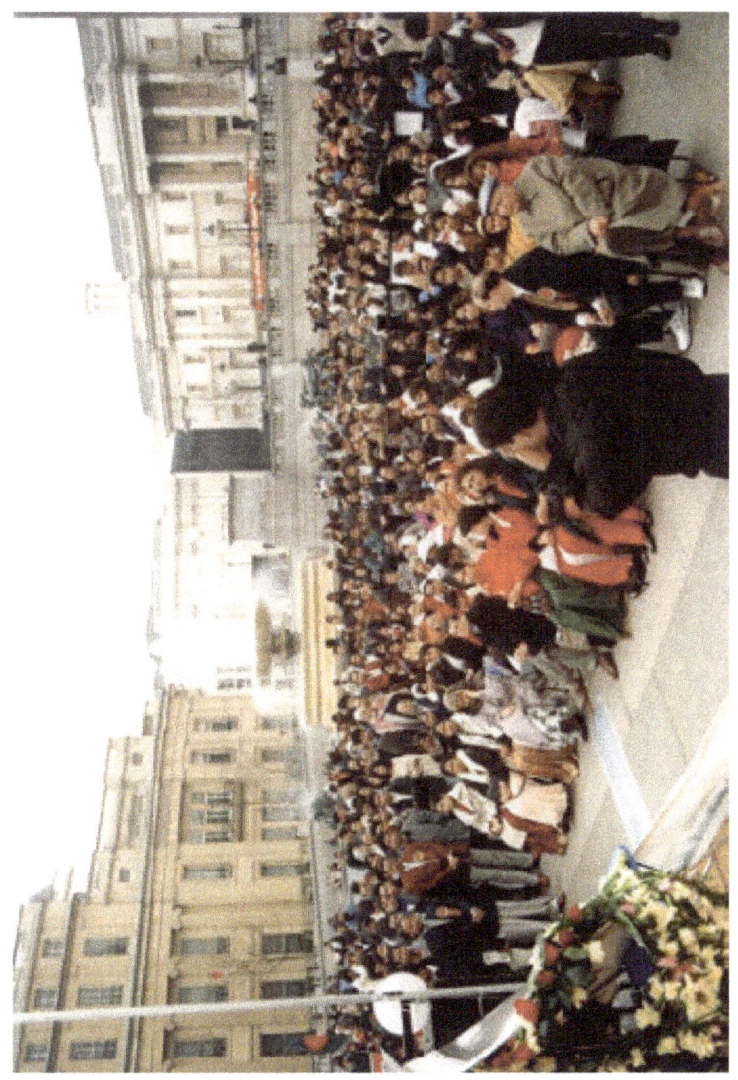

Cameraman

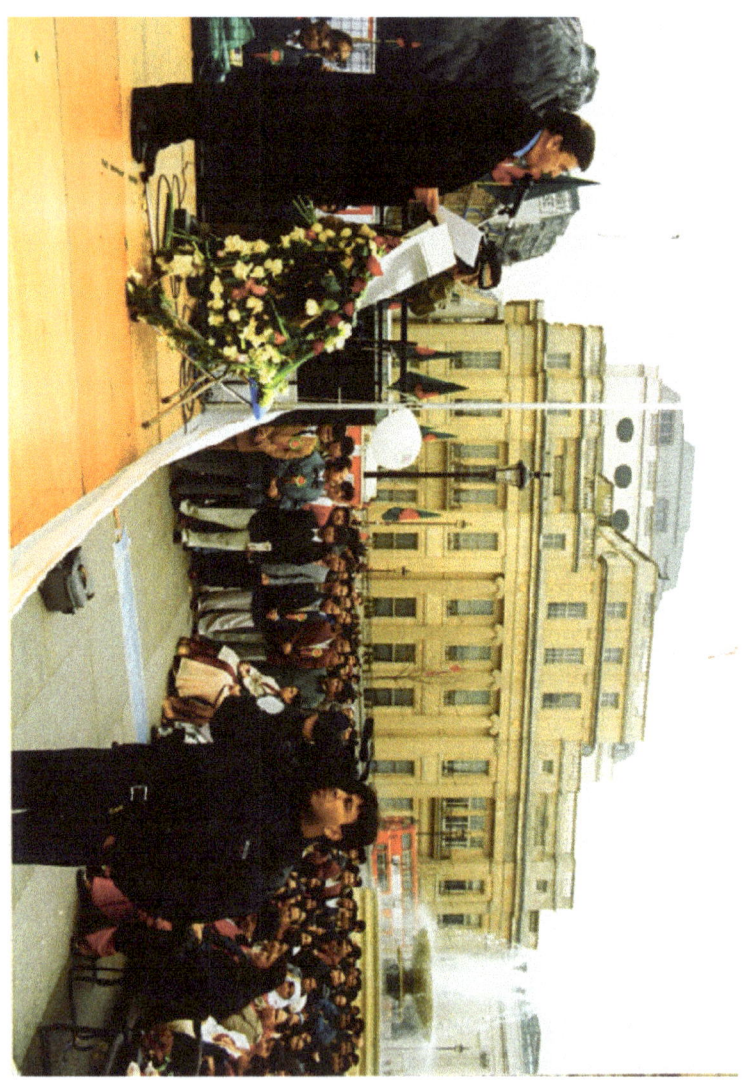

25th Anniversary of Bangladesh in Trafalgar Squares

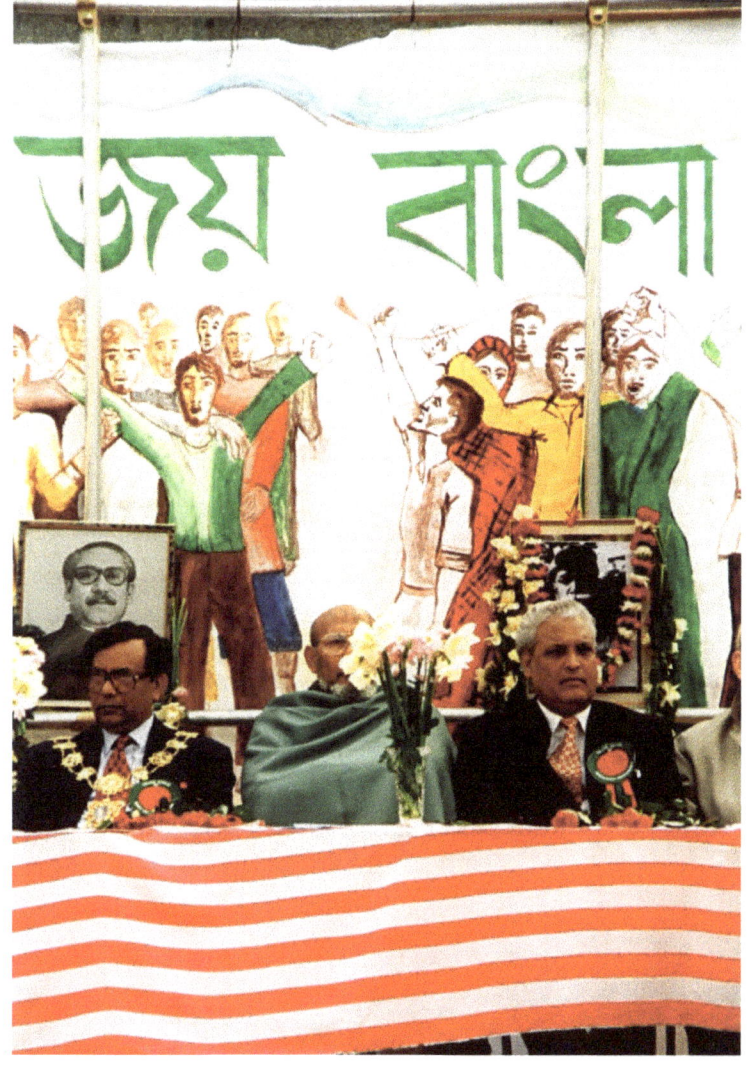

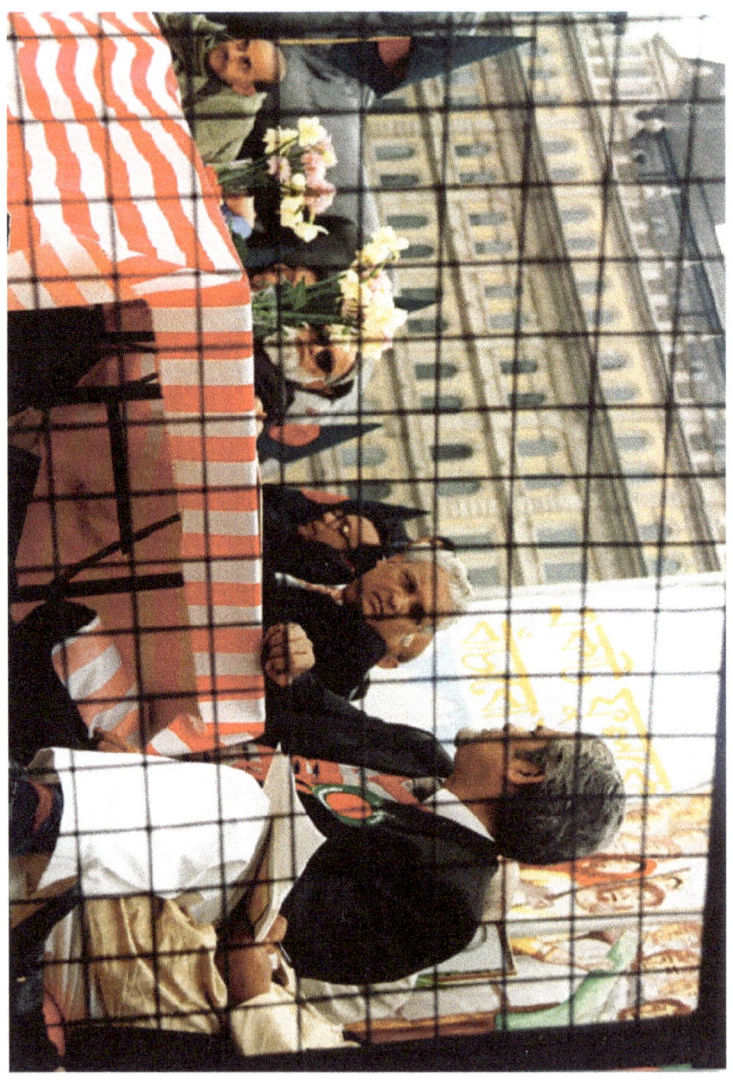

25th Anniversary of Bangladesh in Trafalgar Squares

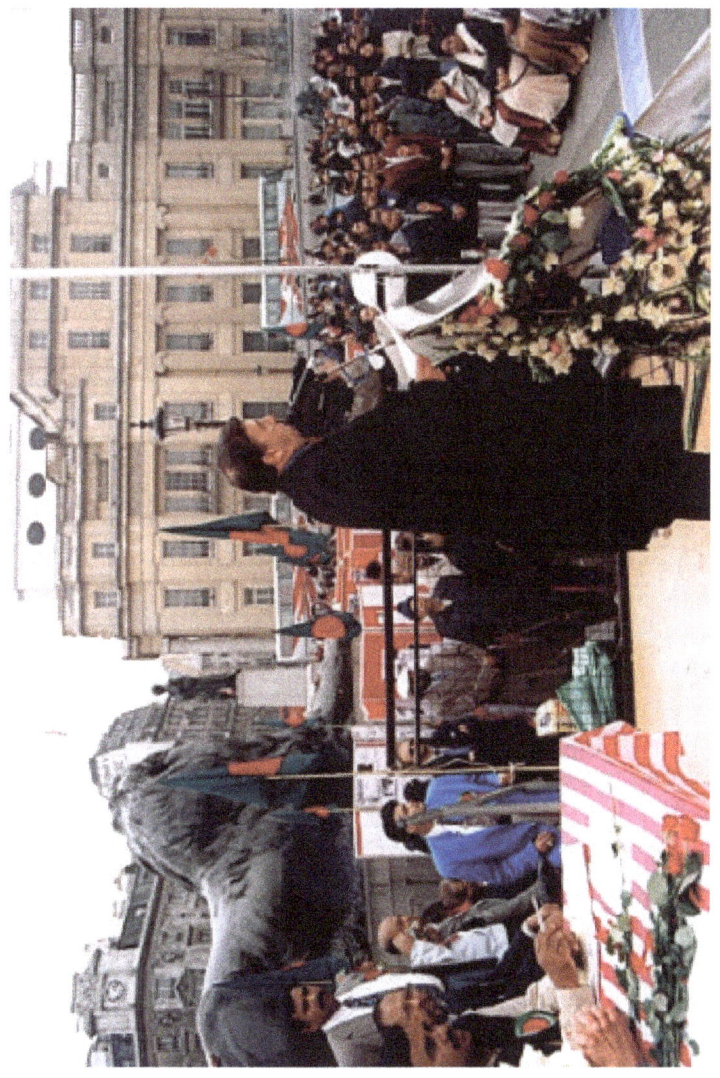

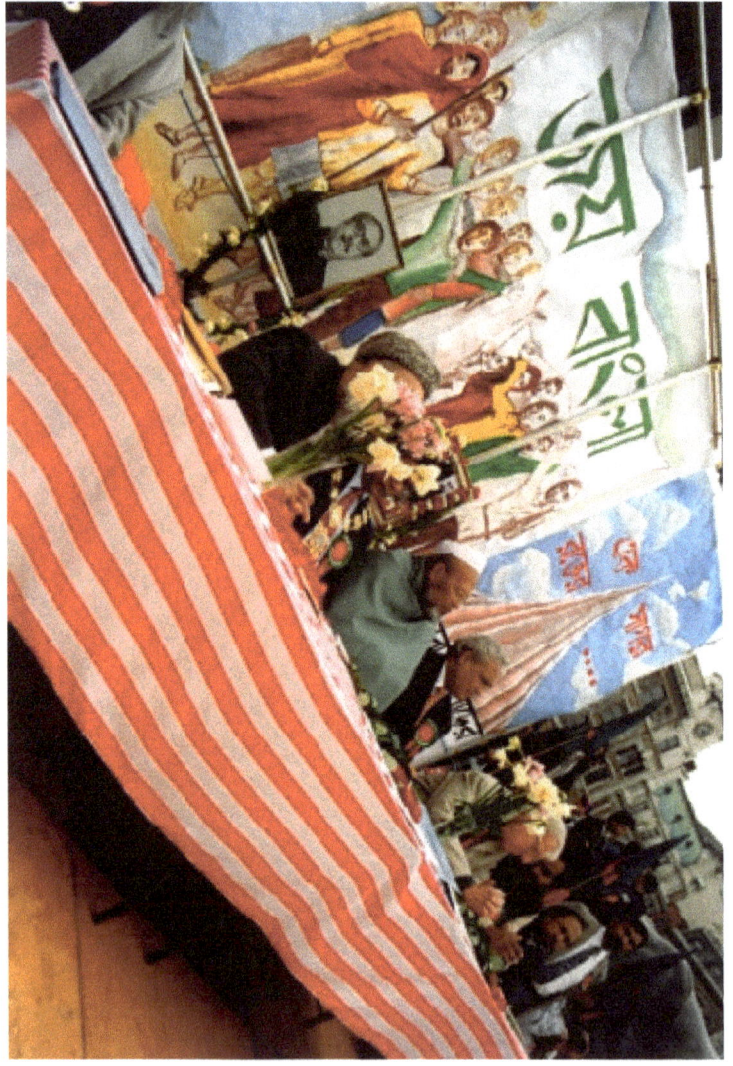

25th Anniversary of Bangladesh in Trafalgar Squares

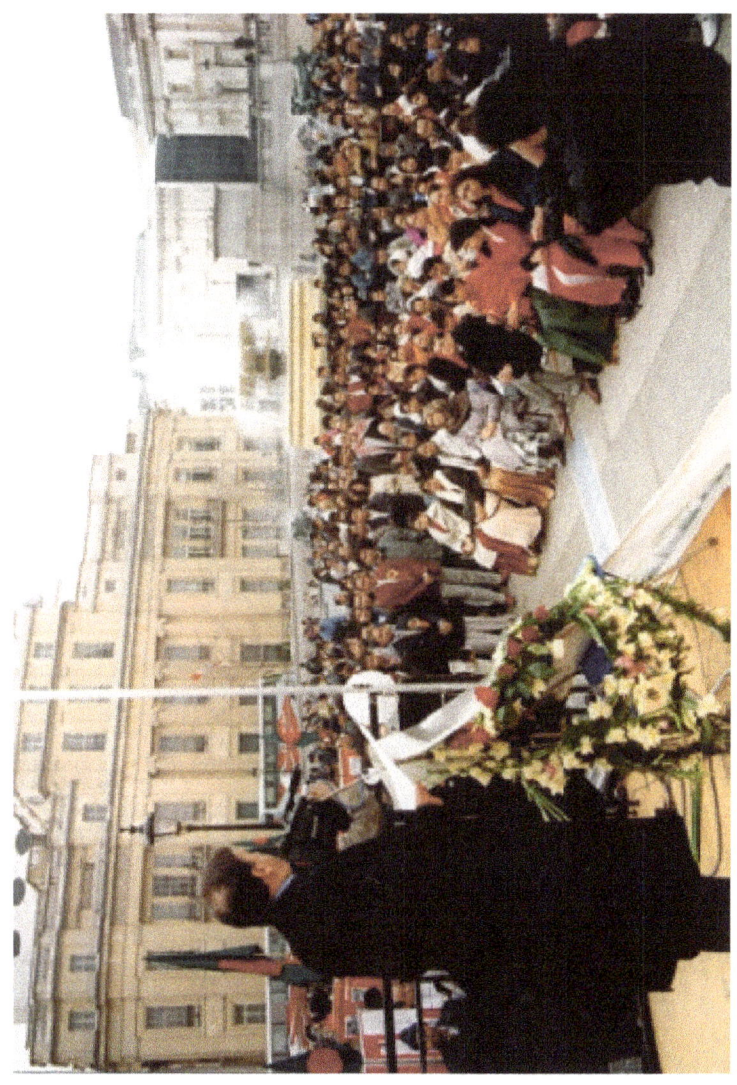

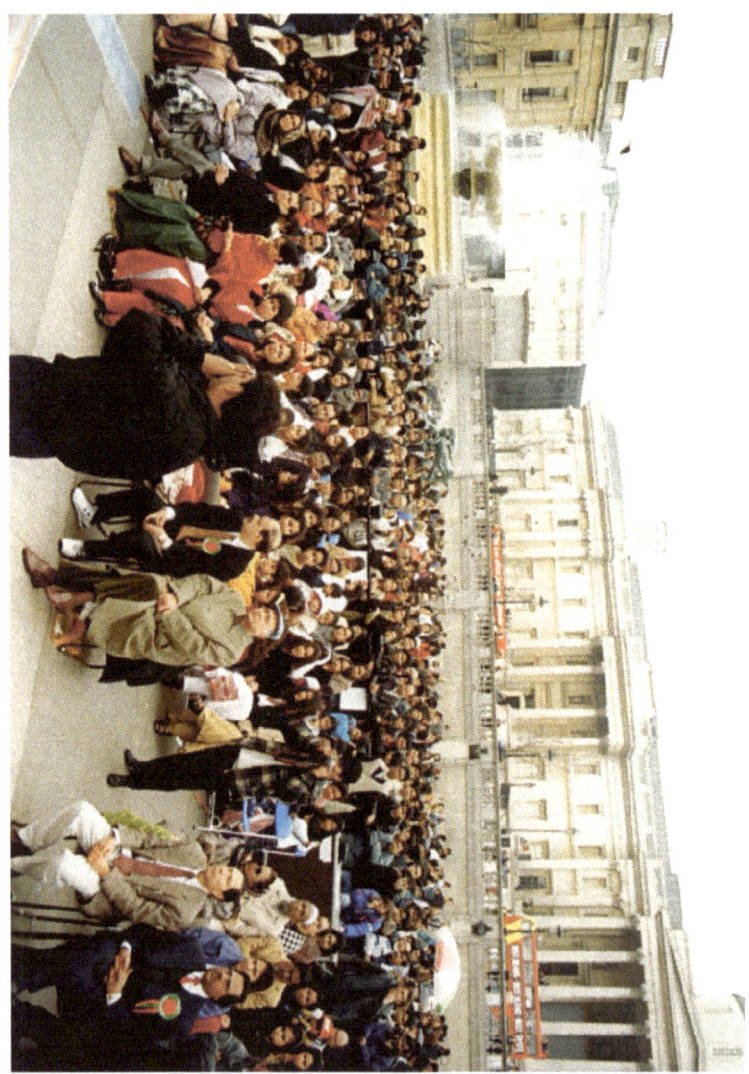

25th Anniversary of Bangladesh in Trafalgar Squares

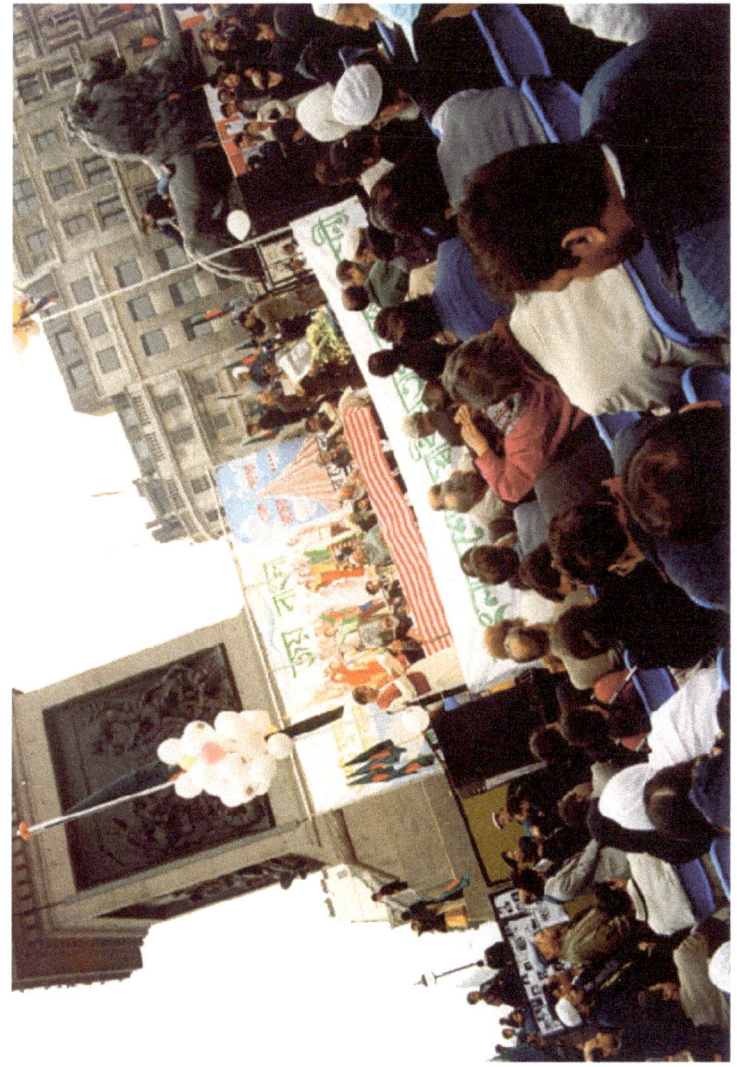

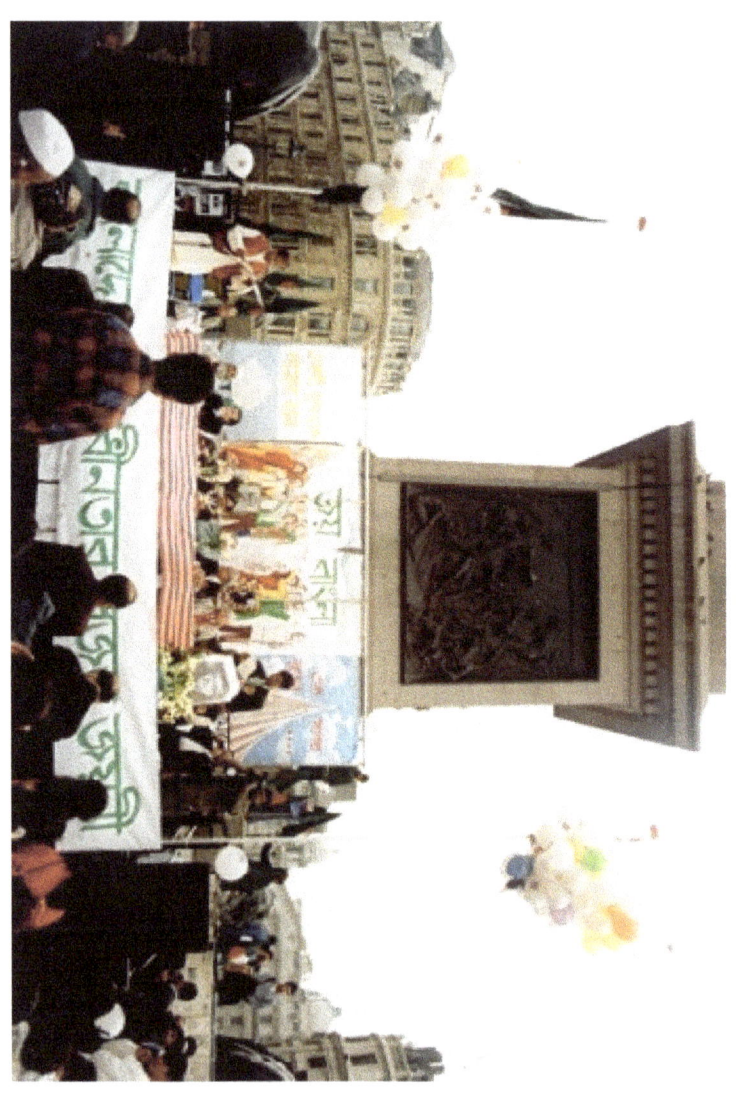

25th Anniversary of Bangladesh in Trafalgar Squares

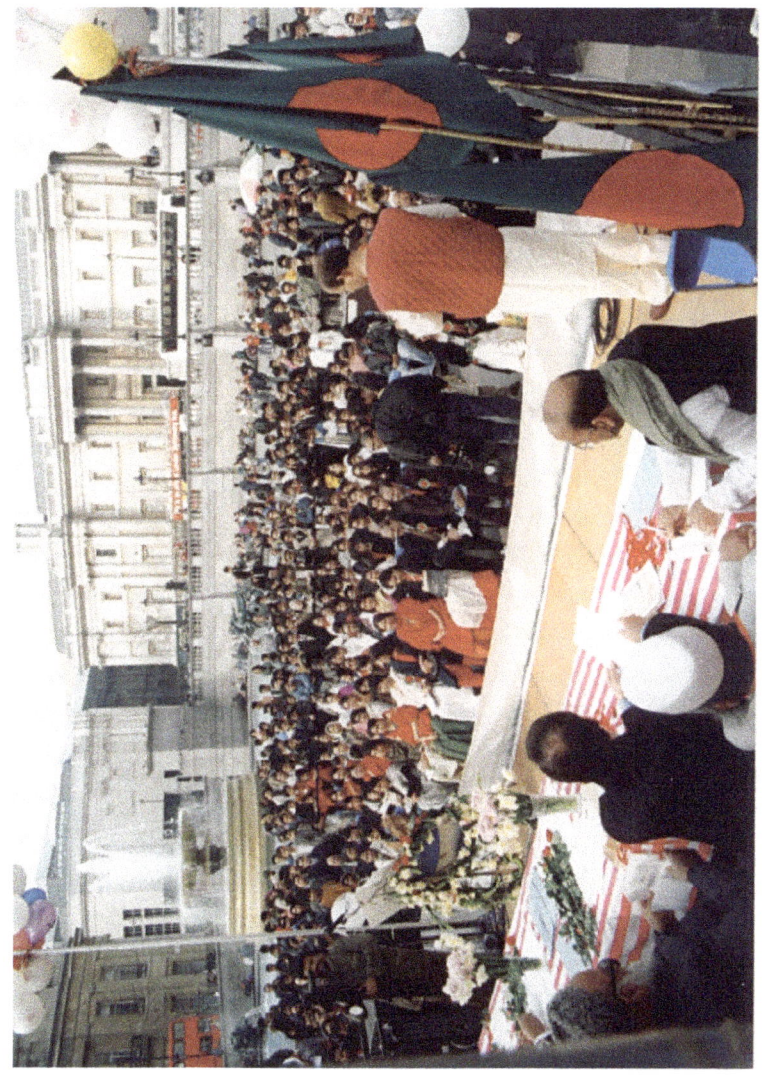

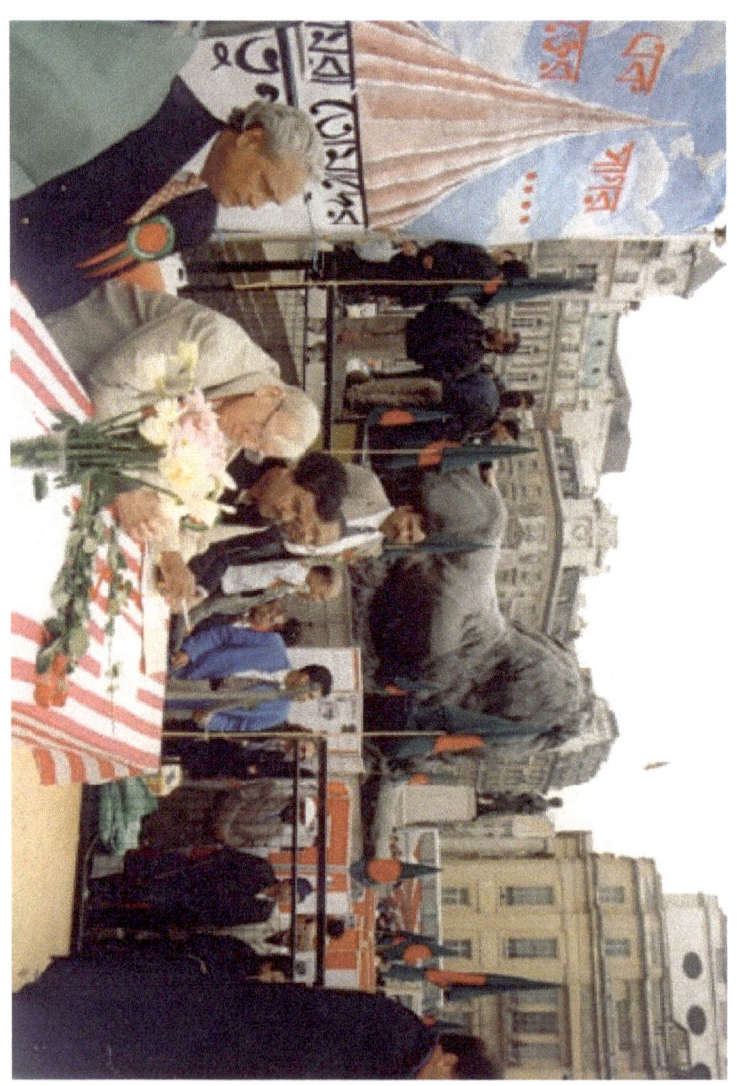

25th Anniversary of Bangladesh in Trafalgar Squares

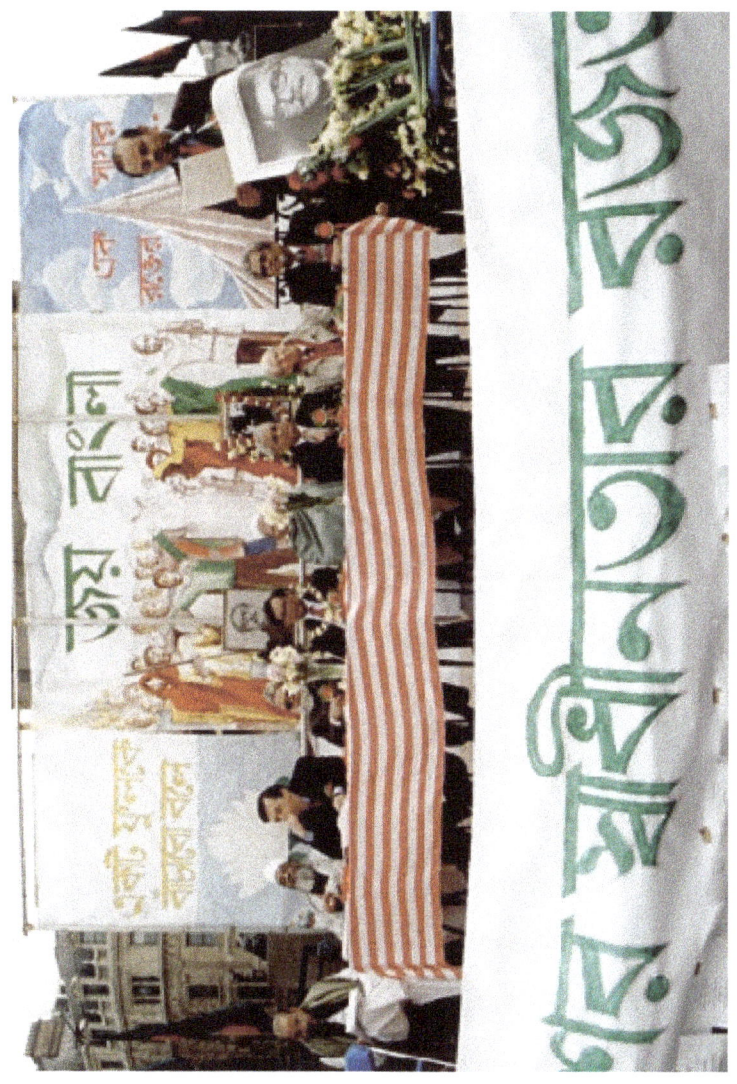

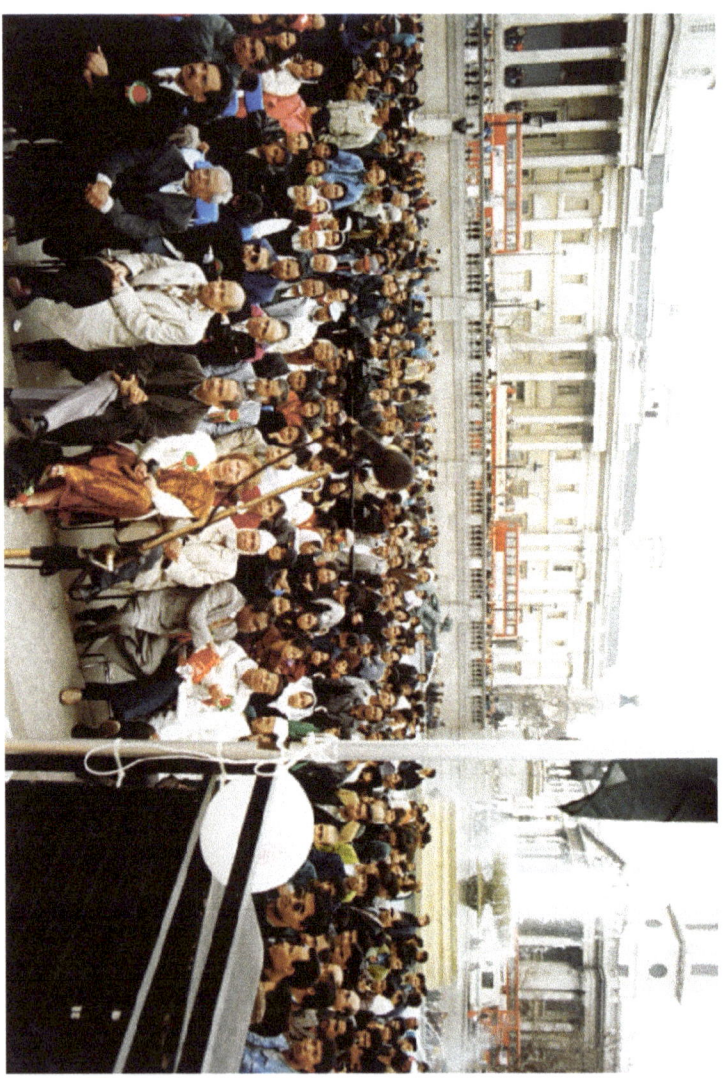

25th Anniversary of Bangladesh in Trafalgar Squares

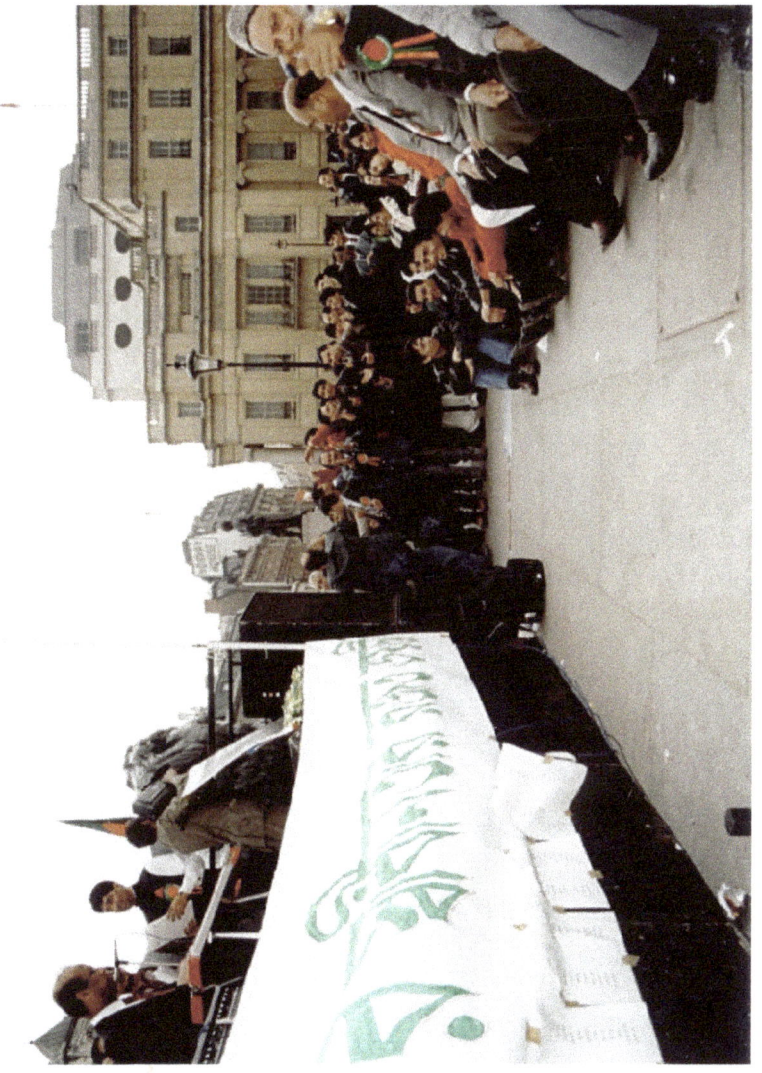

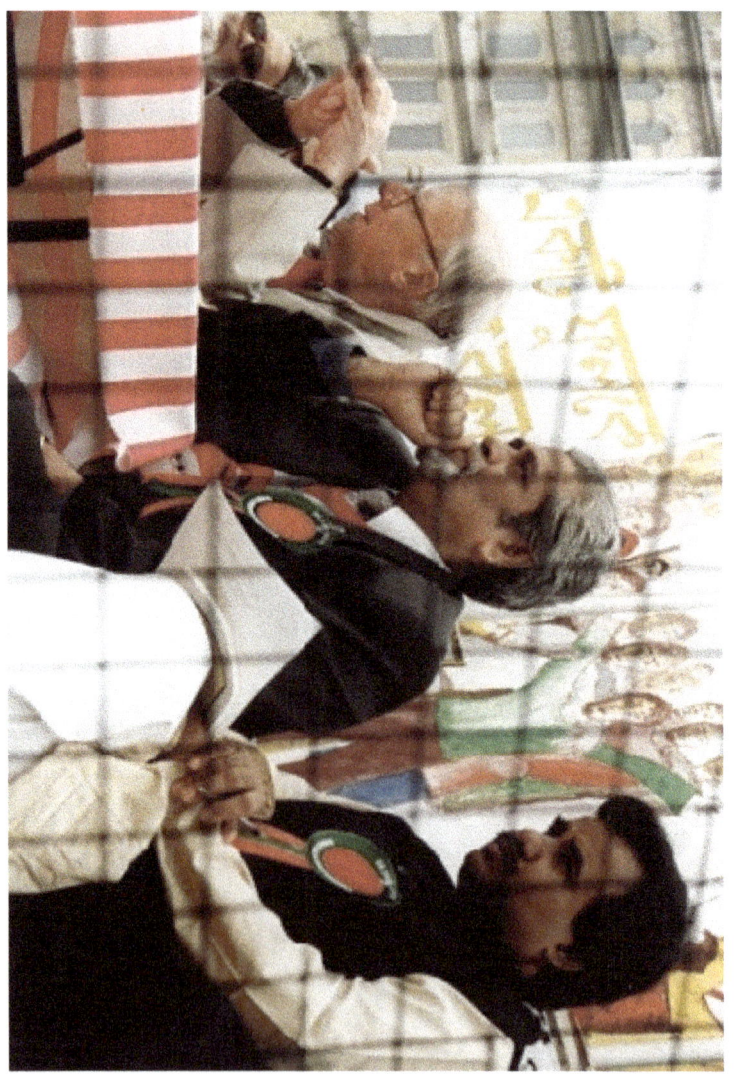

25th Anniversary of Bangladesh in Trafalgar Squares

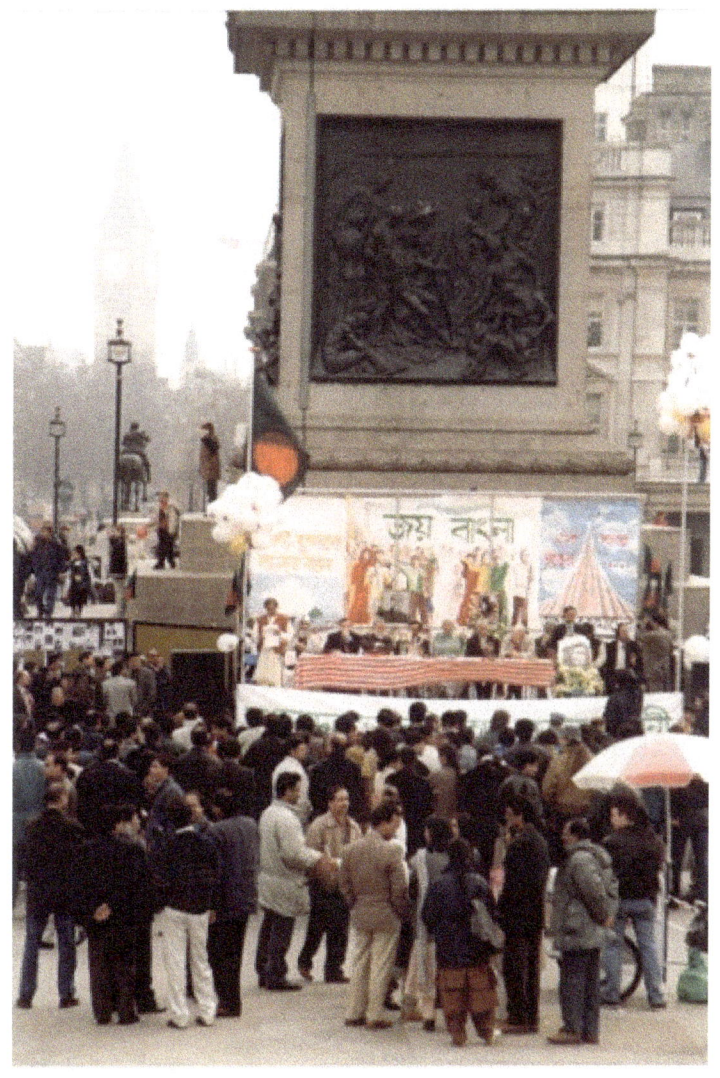

View from the crowd.

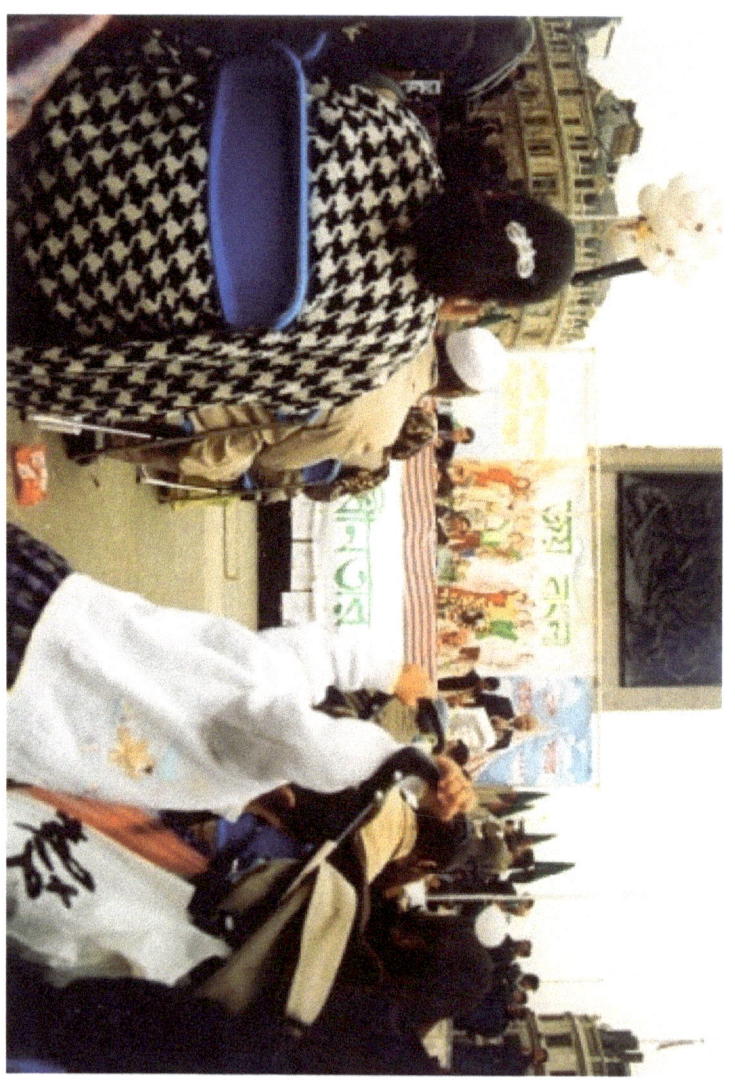

25th Anniversary of Bangladesh in Trafalgar Squares

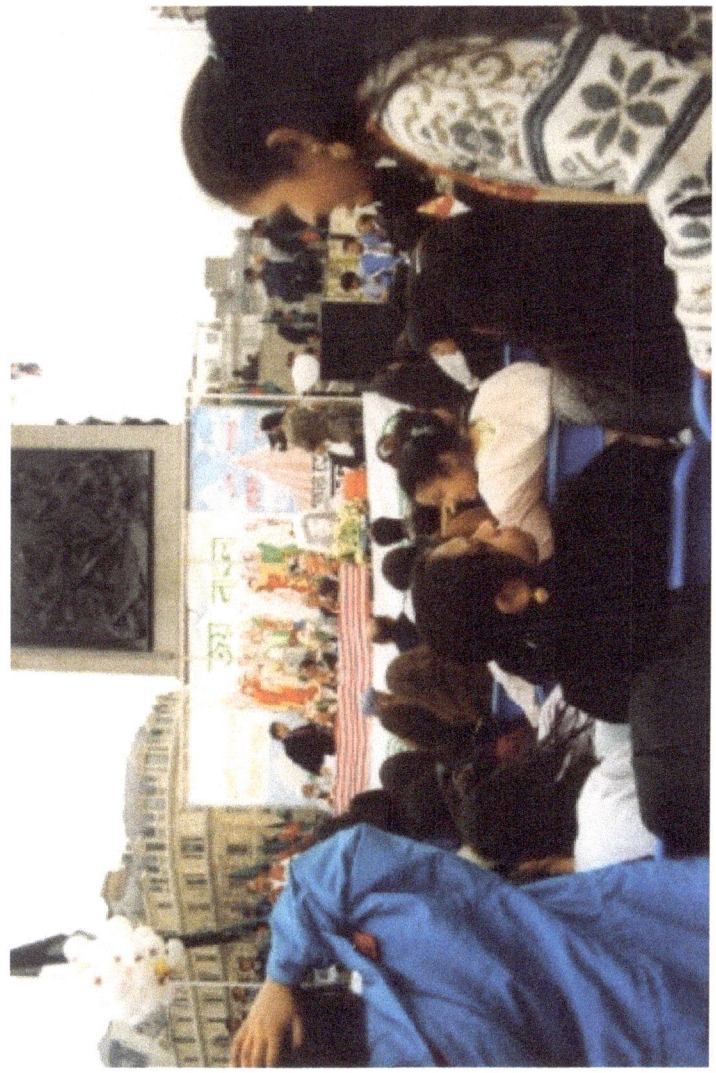

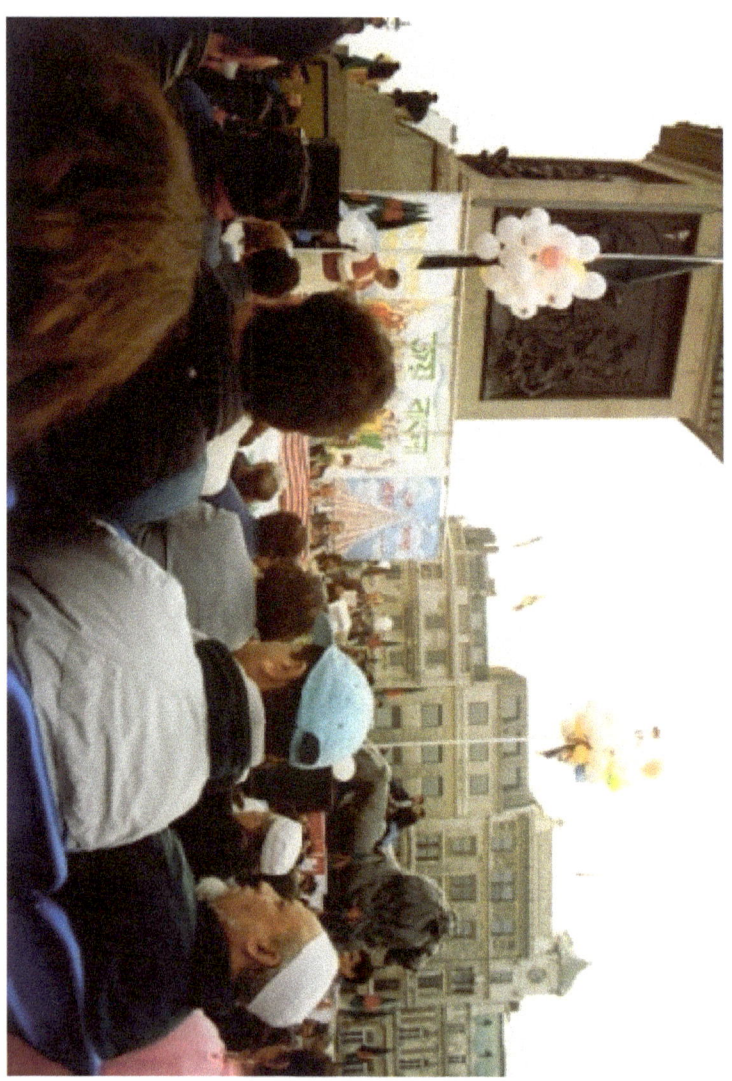

25th Anniversary of Bangladesh in Trafalgar Squares

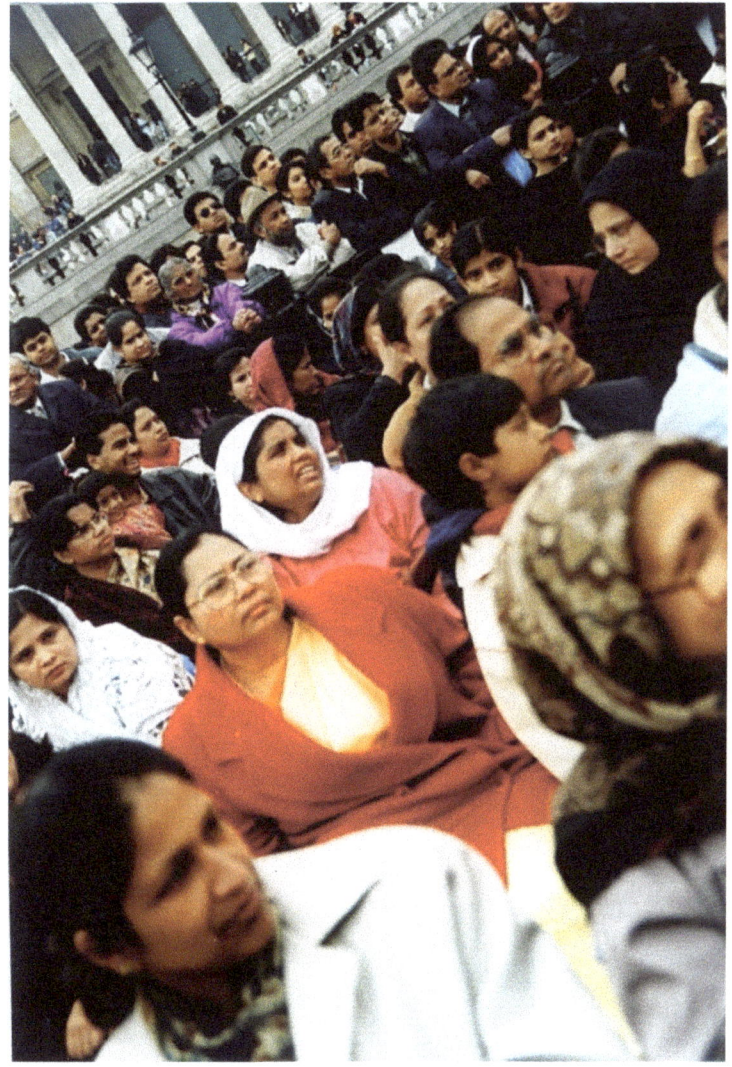

The chosen one on the day

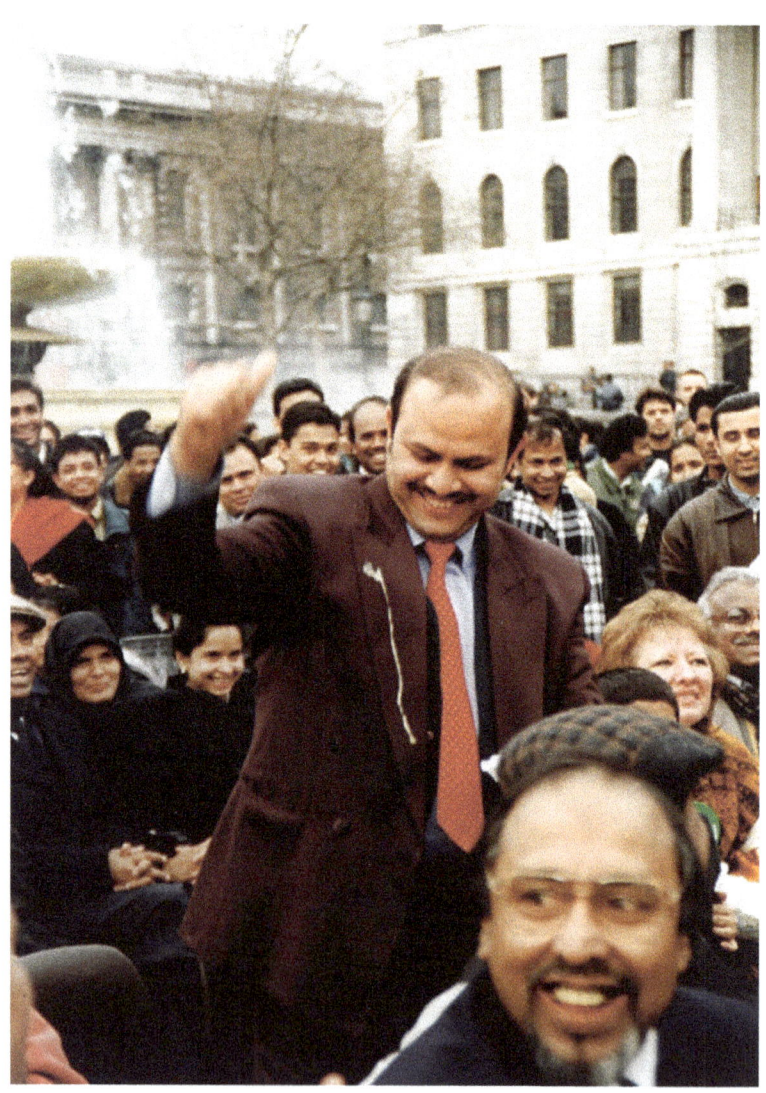

25th Anniversary of Bangladesh in Trafalgar Squares

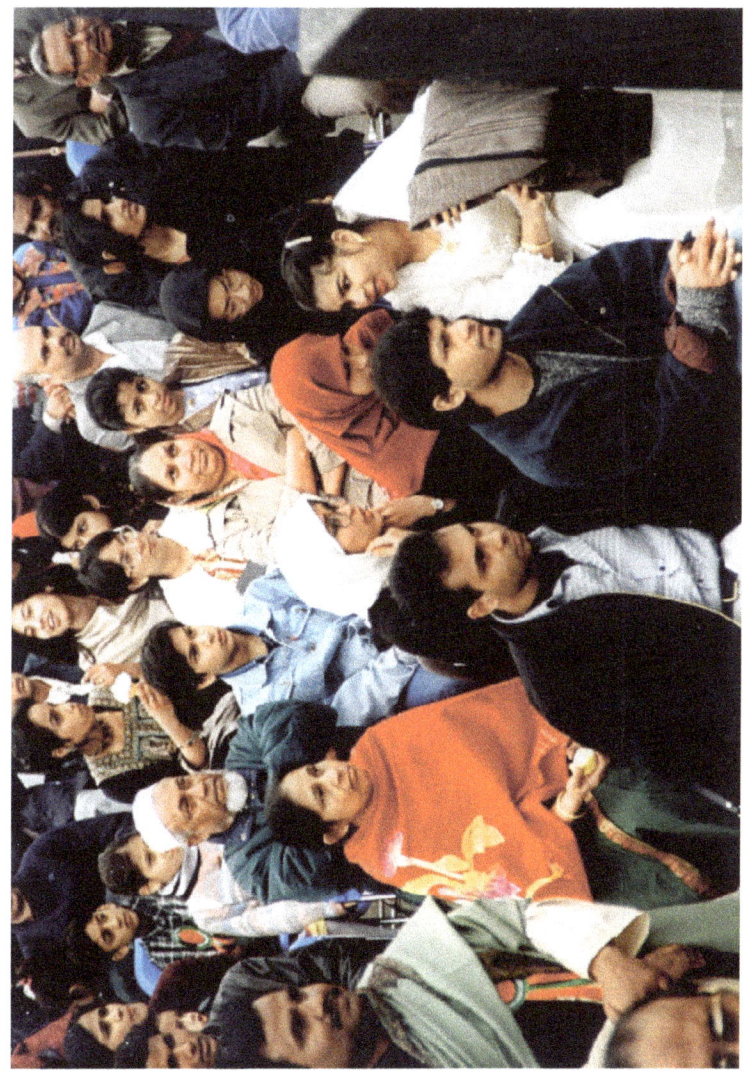

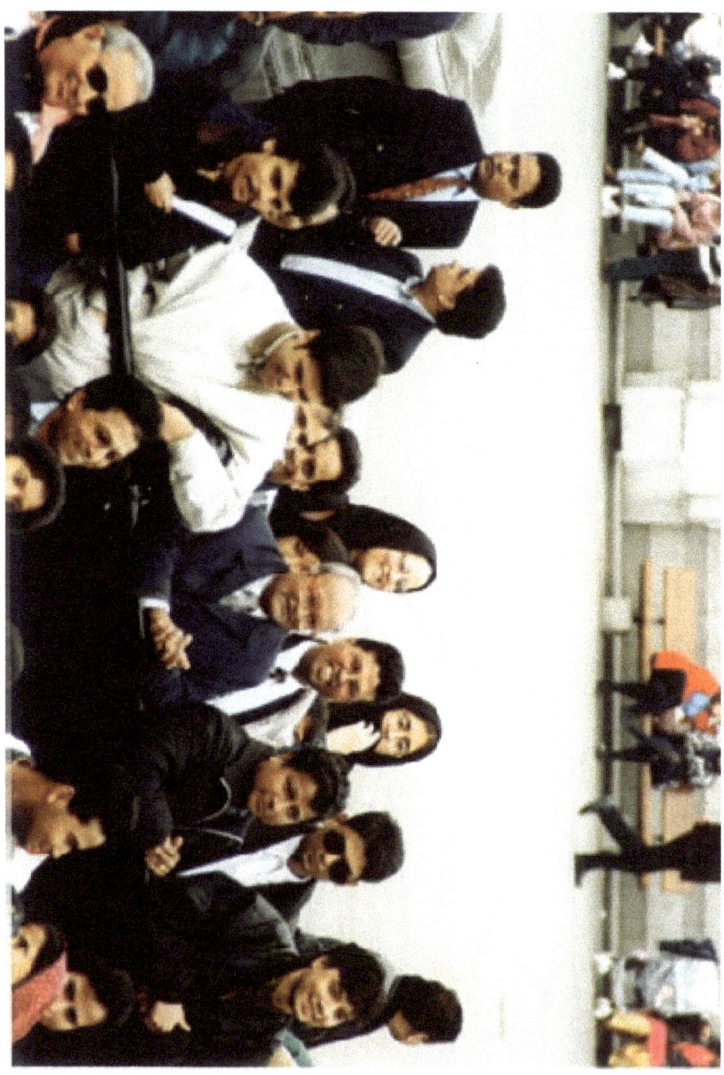

25th Anniversary of Bangladesh in Trafalgar Squares

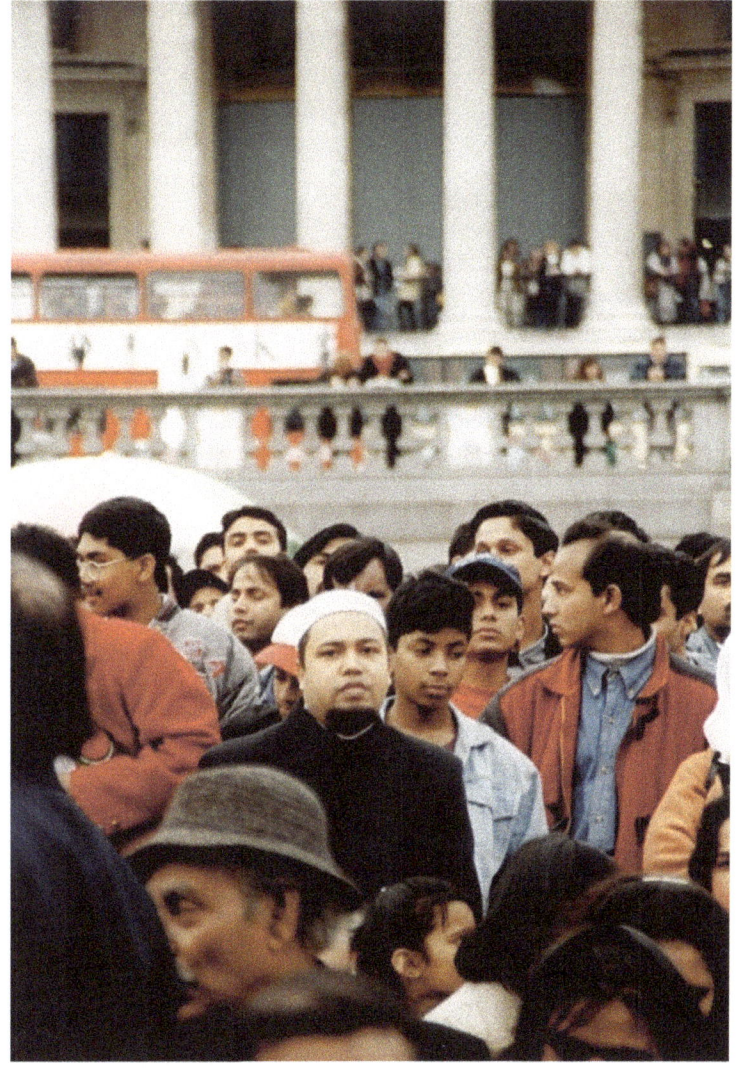

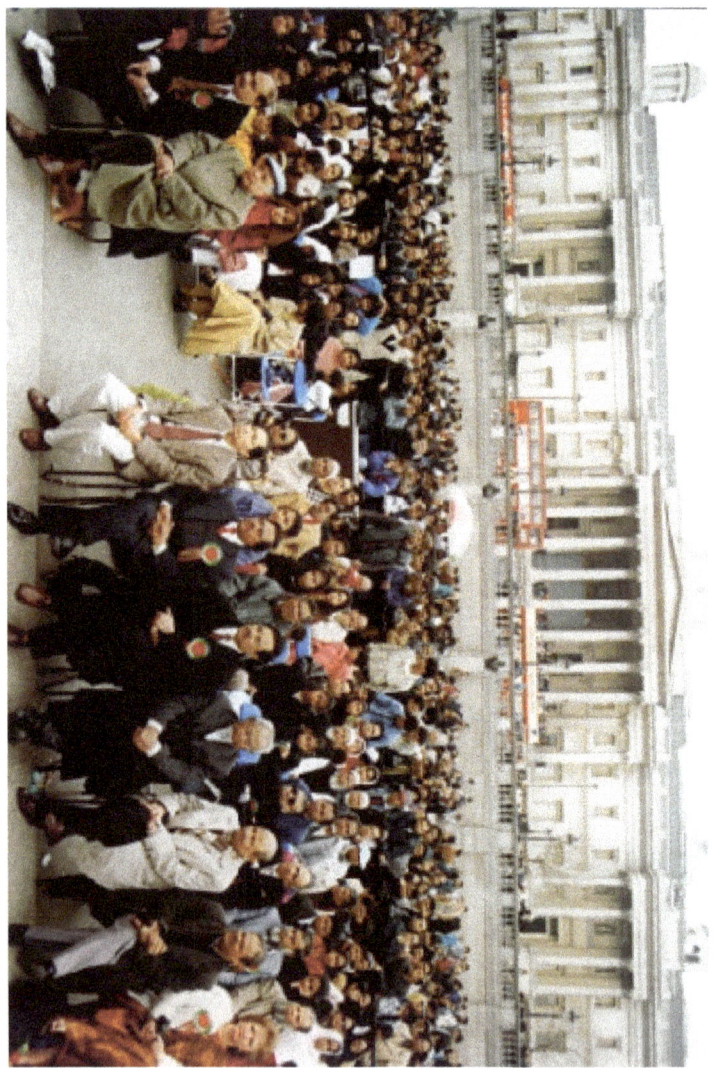

25th Anniversary of Bangladesh in Trafalgar Squares

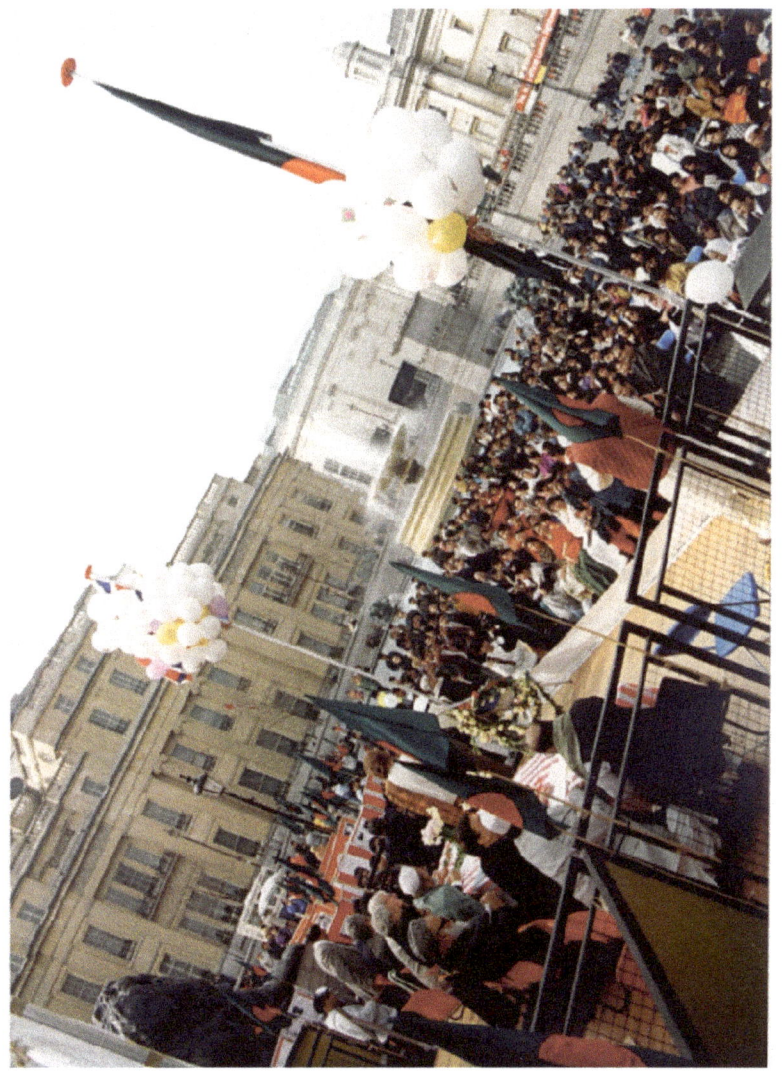

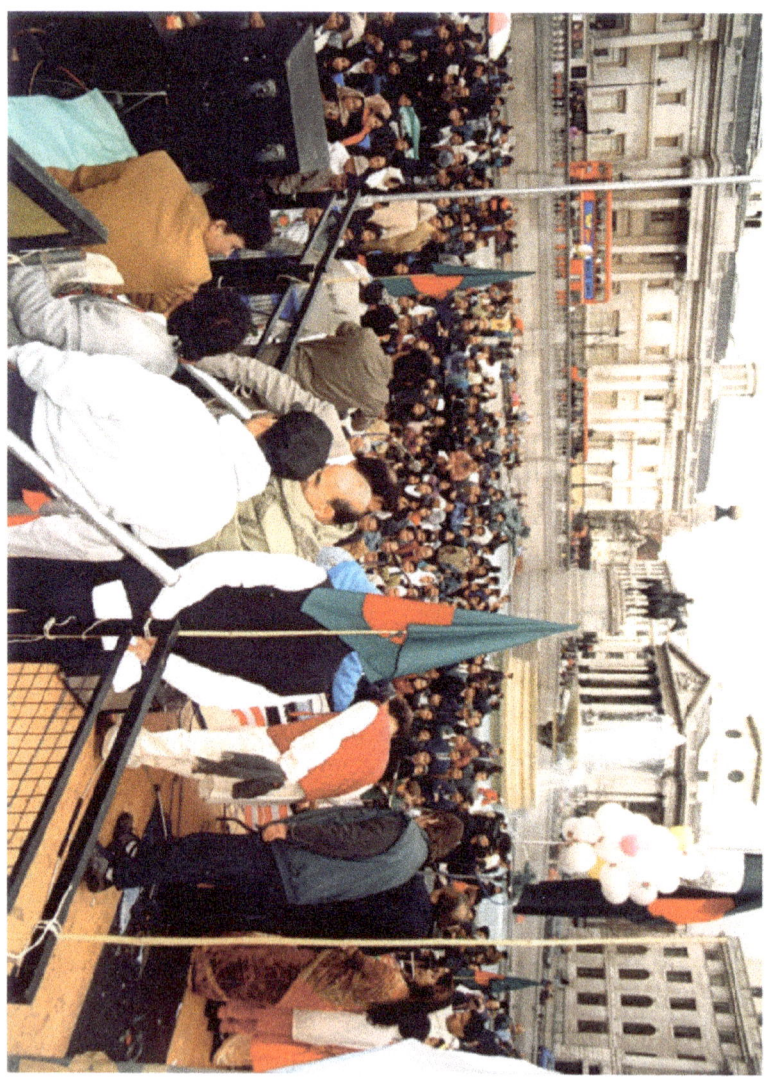

25th Anniversary of Bangladesh in Trafalgar Squares

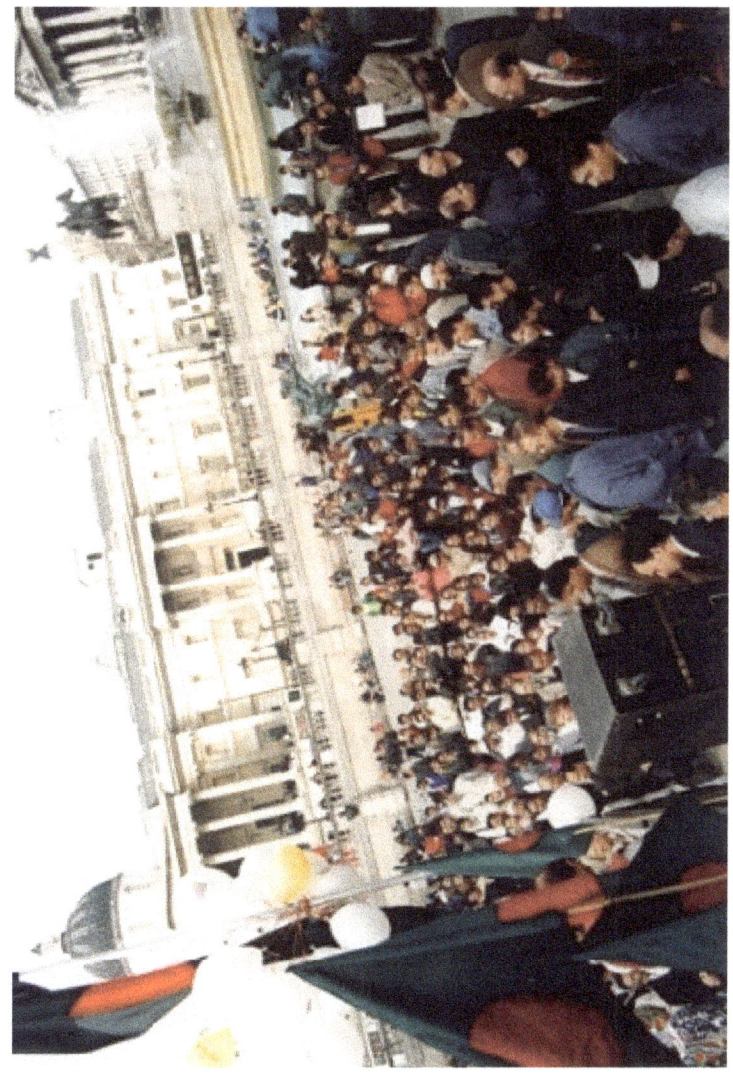

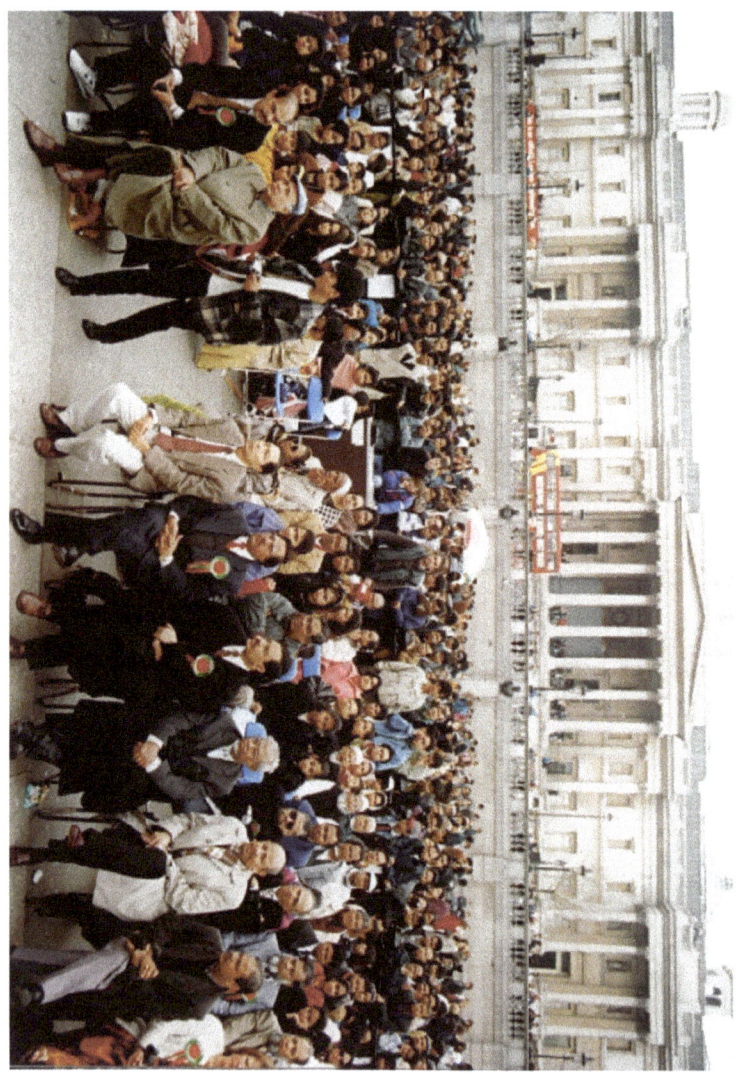

25th Anniversary of Bangladesh in Trafalgar Squares

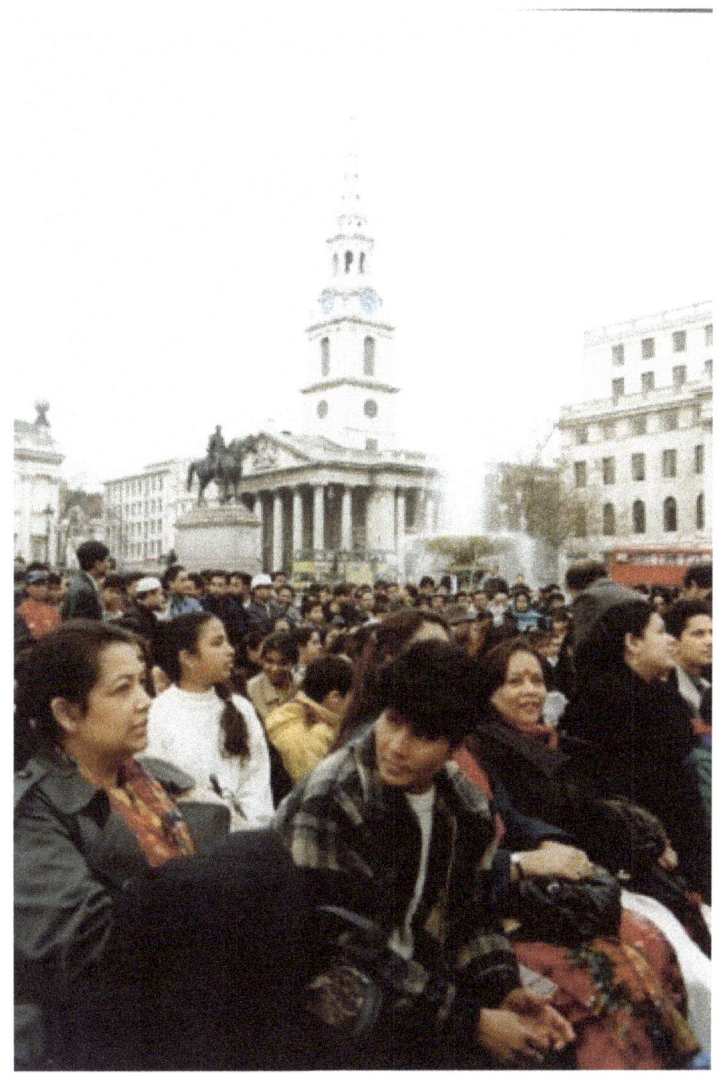

Genocide Exhibition

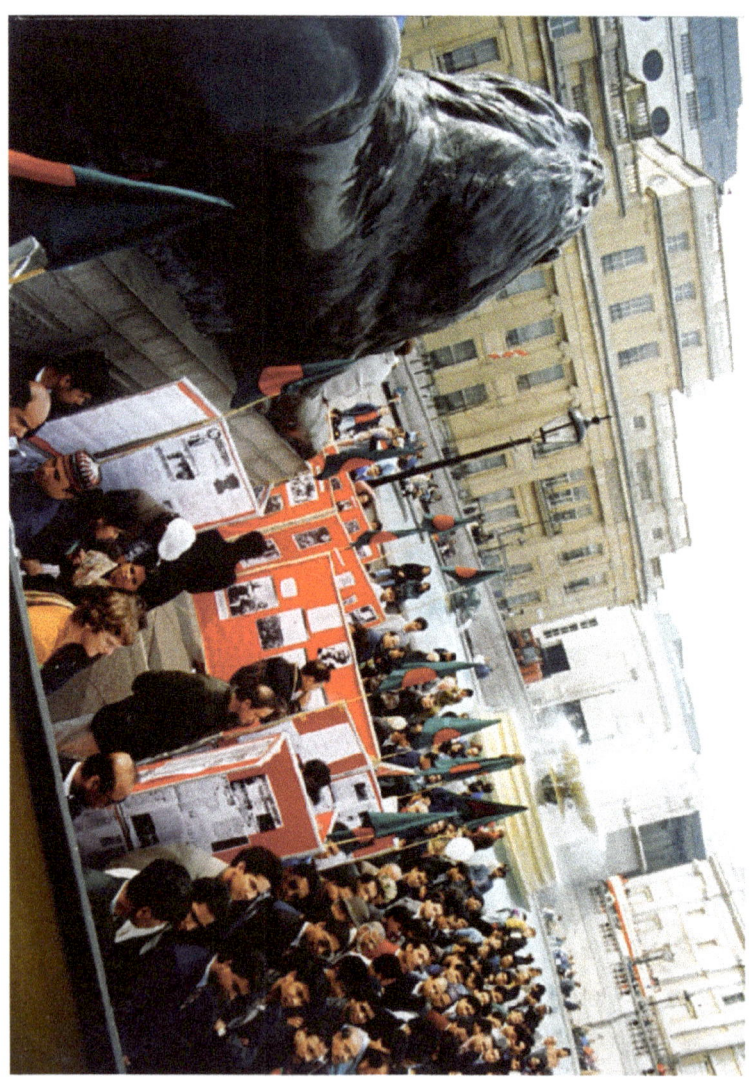

25th Anniversary of Bangladesh in Trafalgar Squares

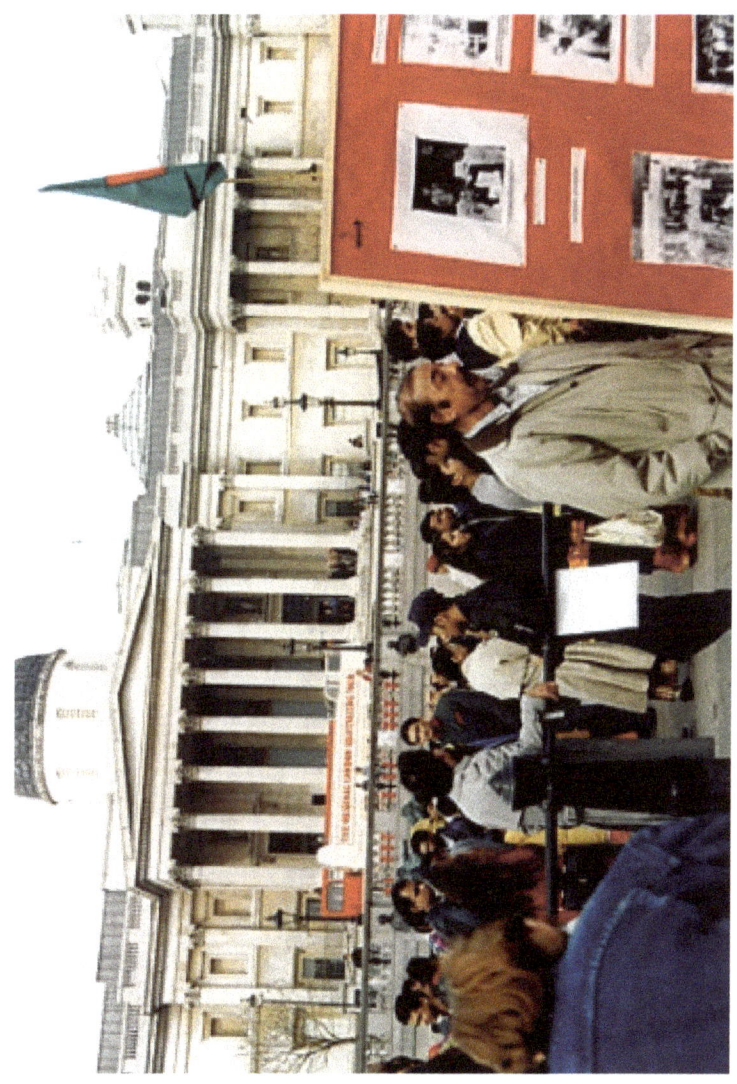

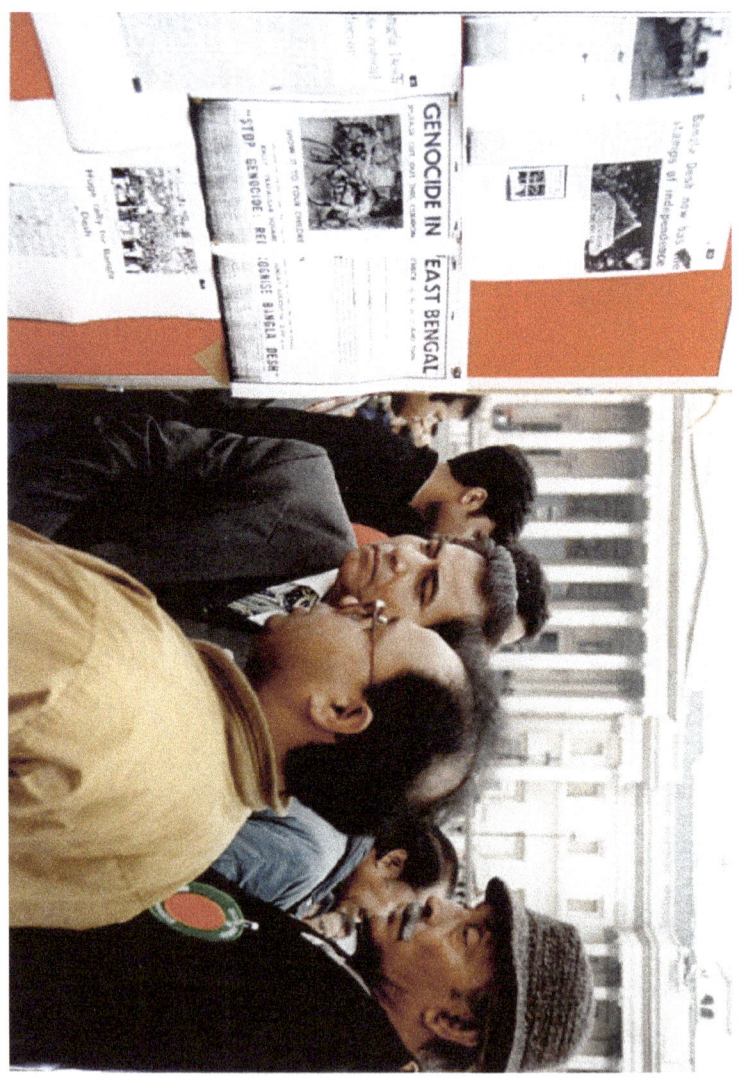

25th Anniversary of Bangladesh in Trafalgar Squares

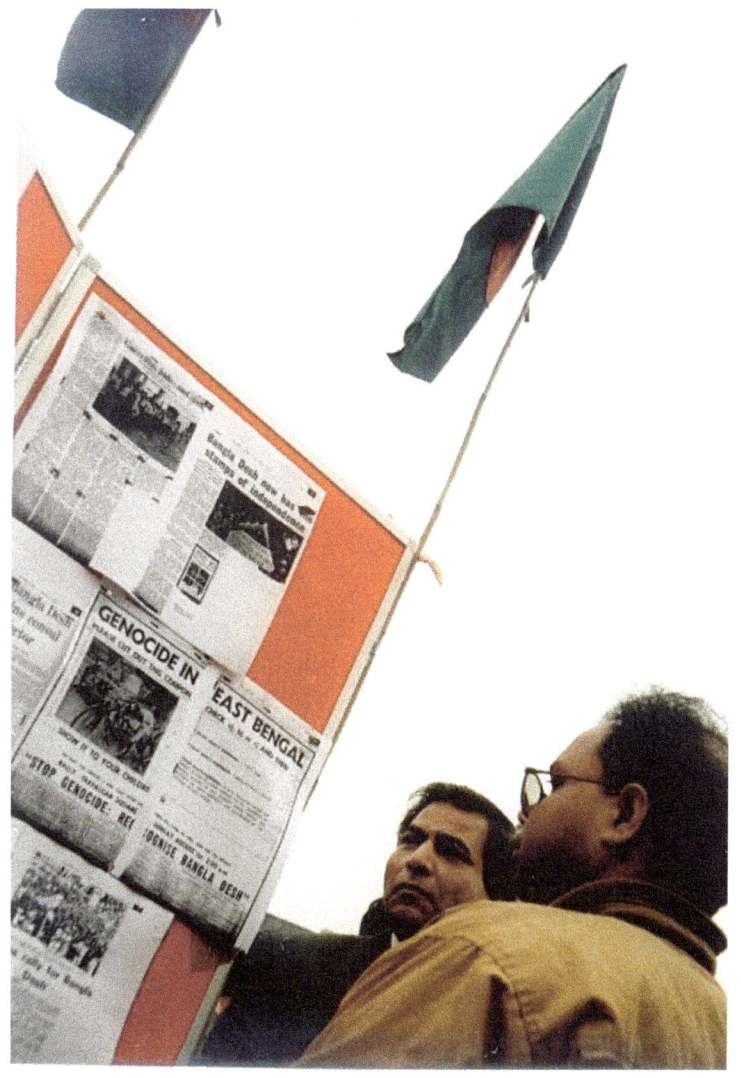

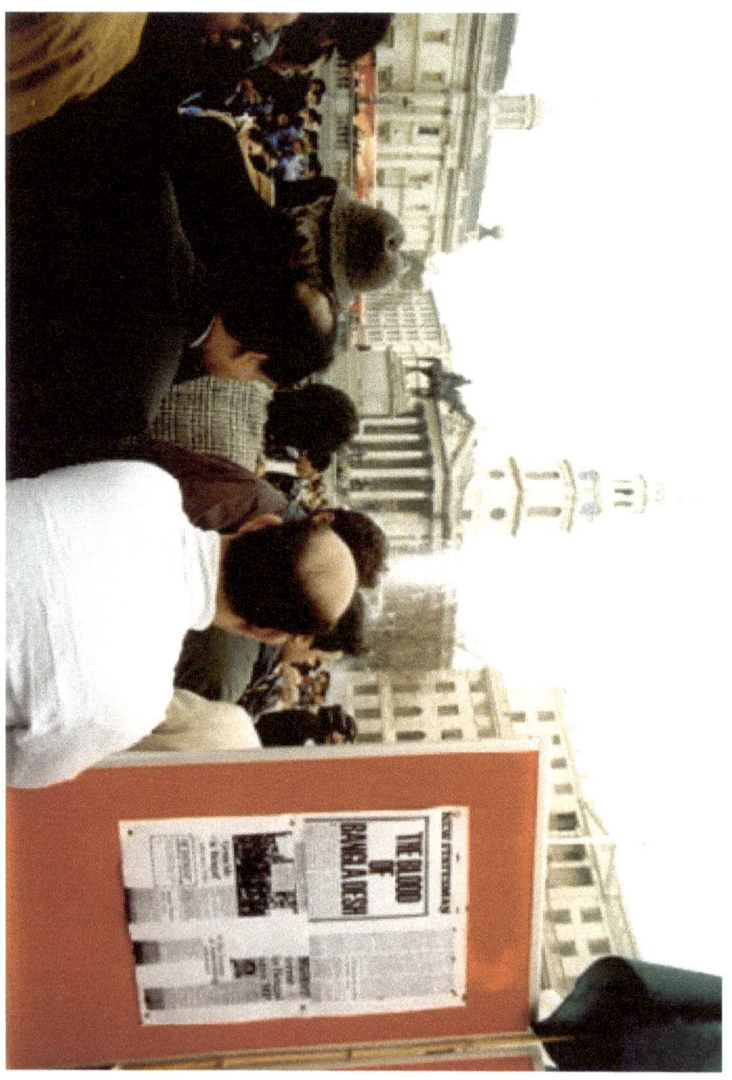

25th Anniversary of Bangladesh in Trafalgar Squares

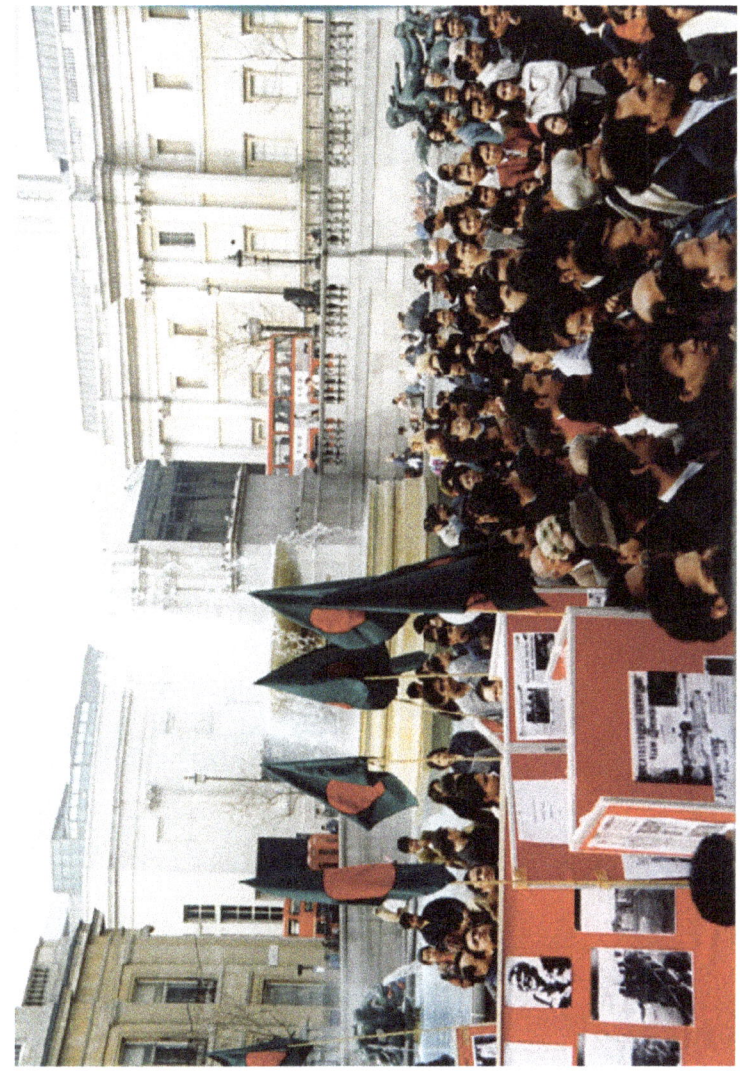

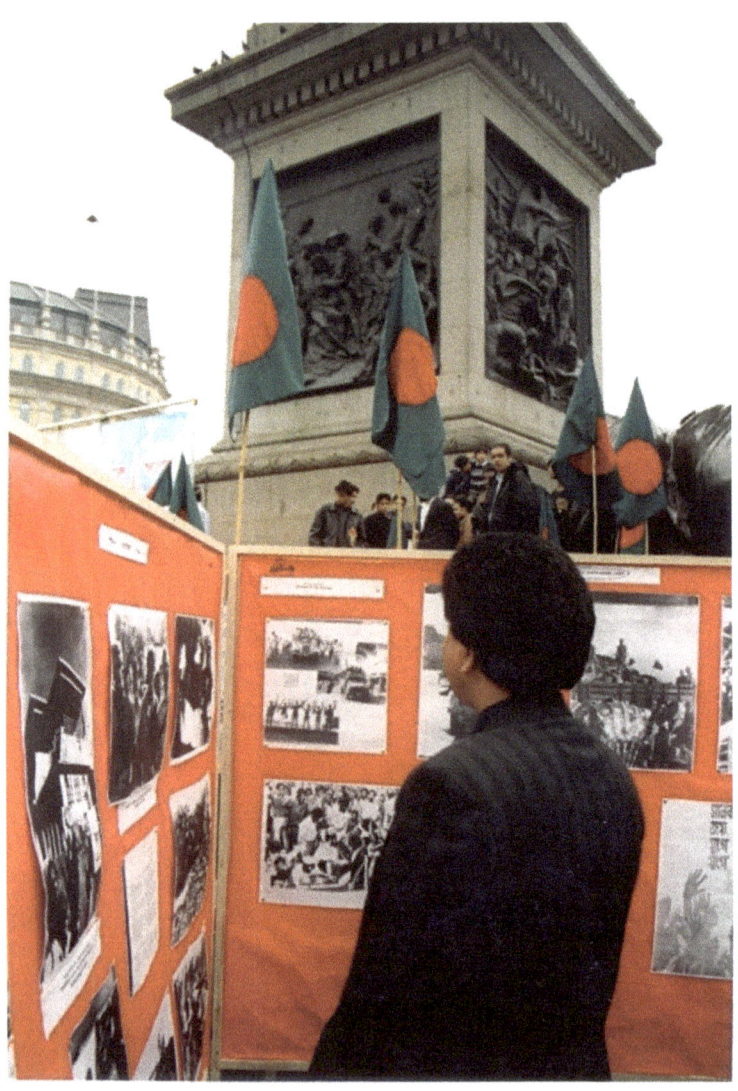

25th Anniversary of Bangladesh in Trafalgar Squares

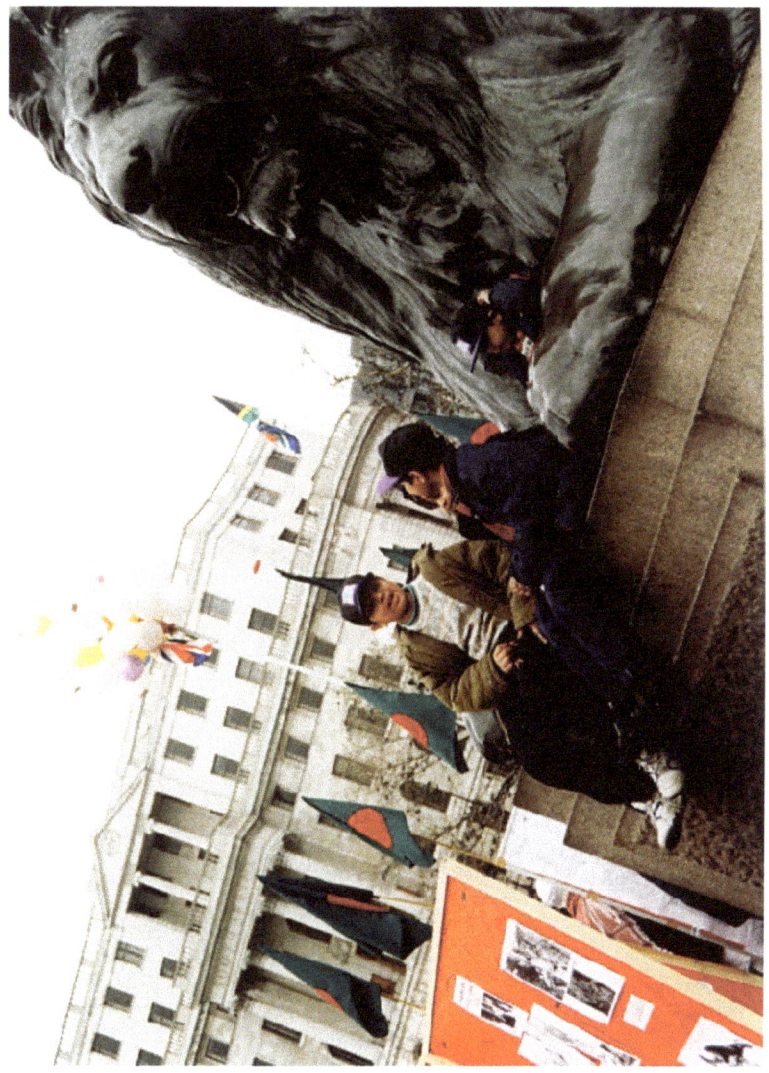

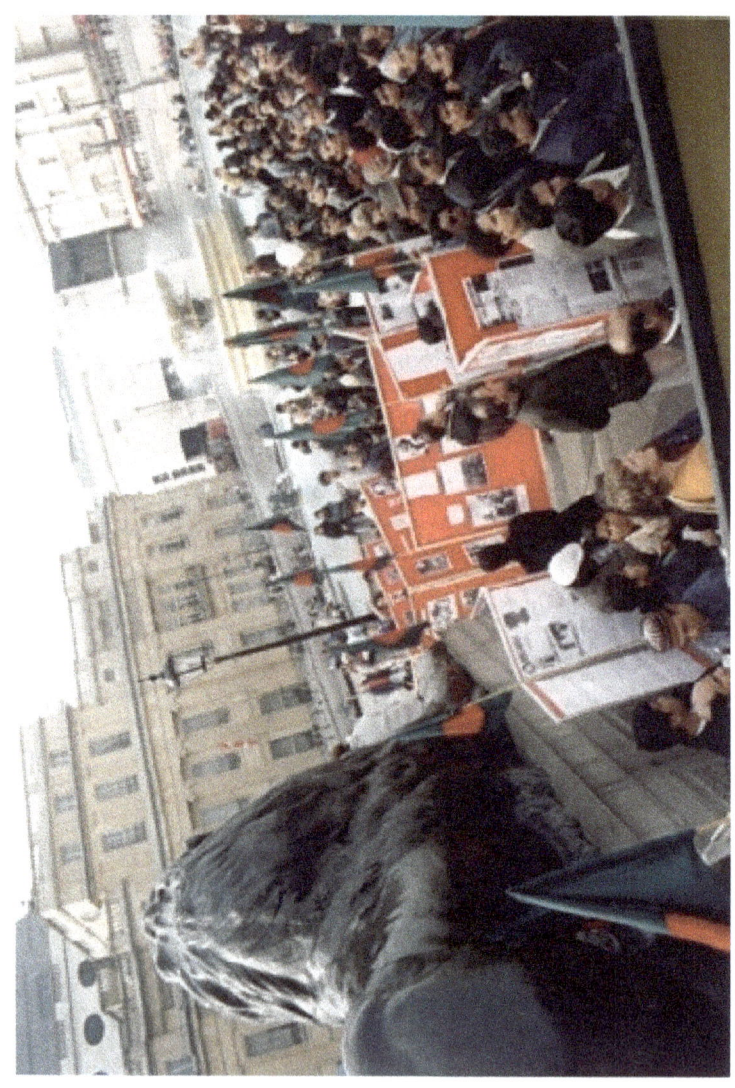

25th Anniversary of Bangladesh in Trafalgar Squares

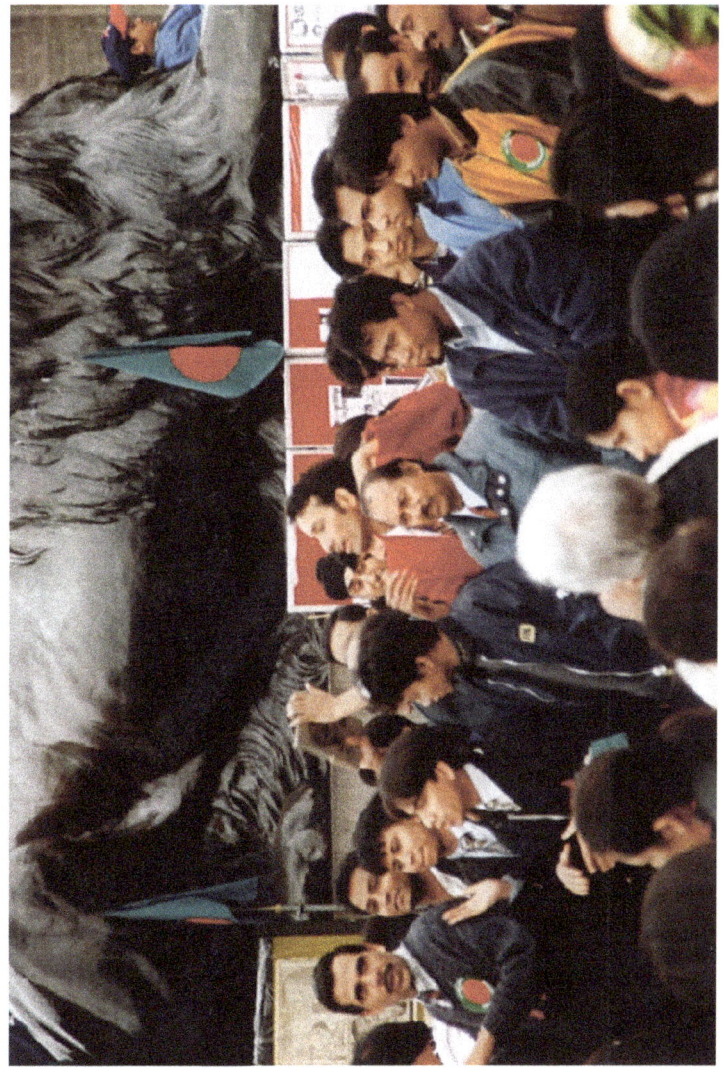

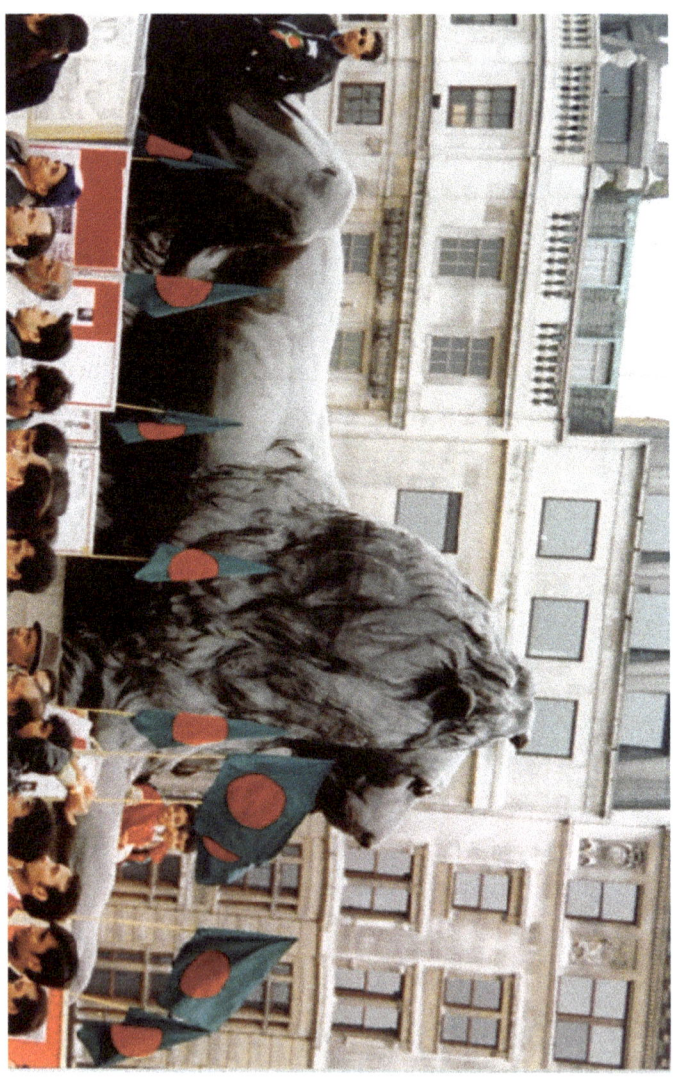

25th Anniversary of Bangladesh in Trafalgar Squares

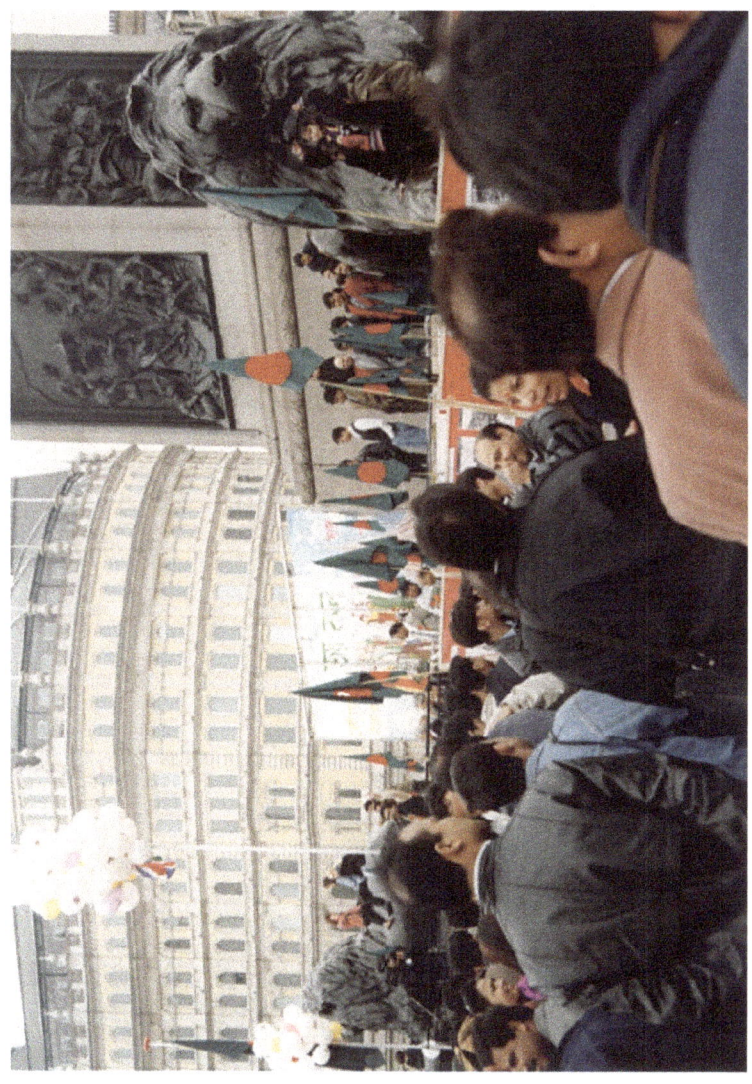

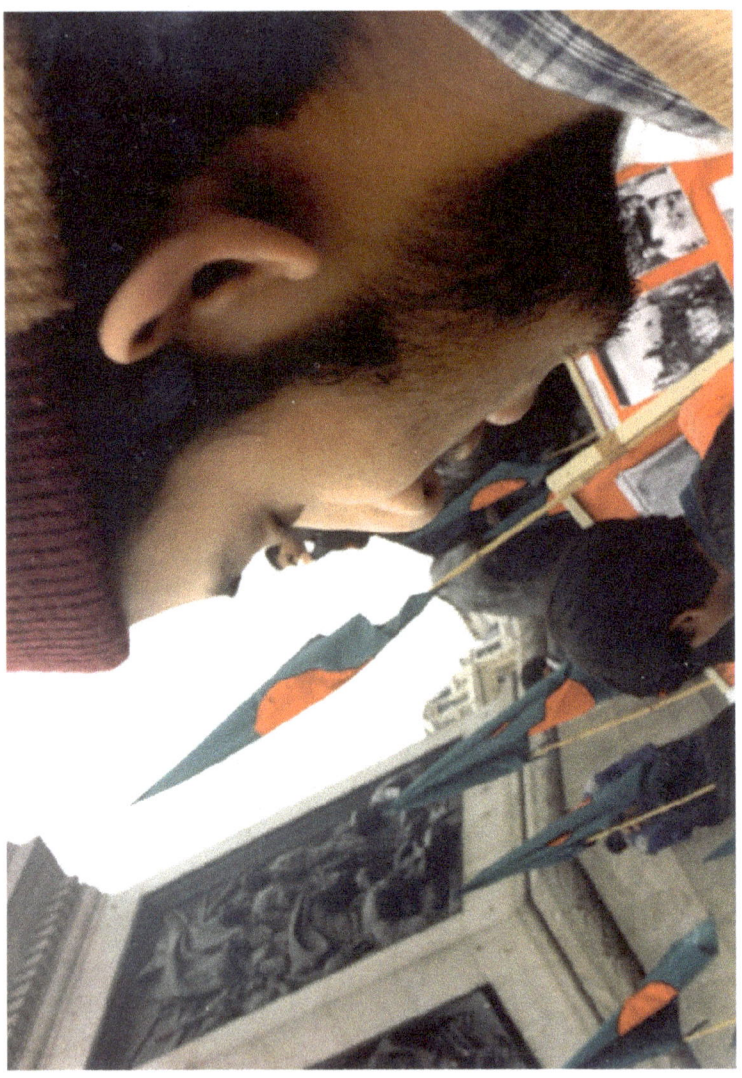

25th Anniversary of Bangladesh in Trafalgar Squares

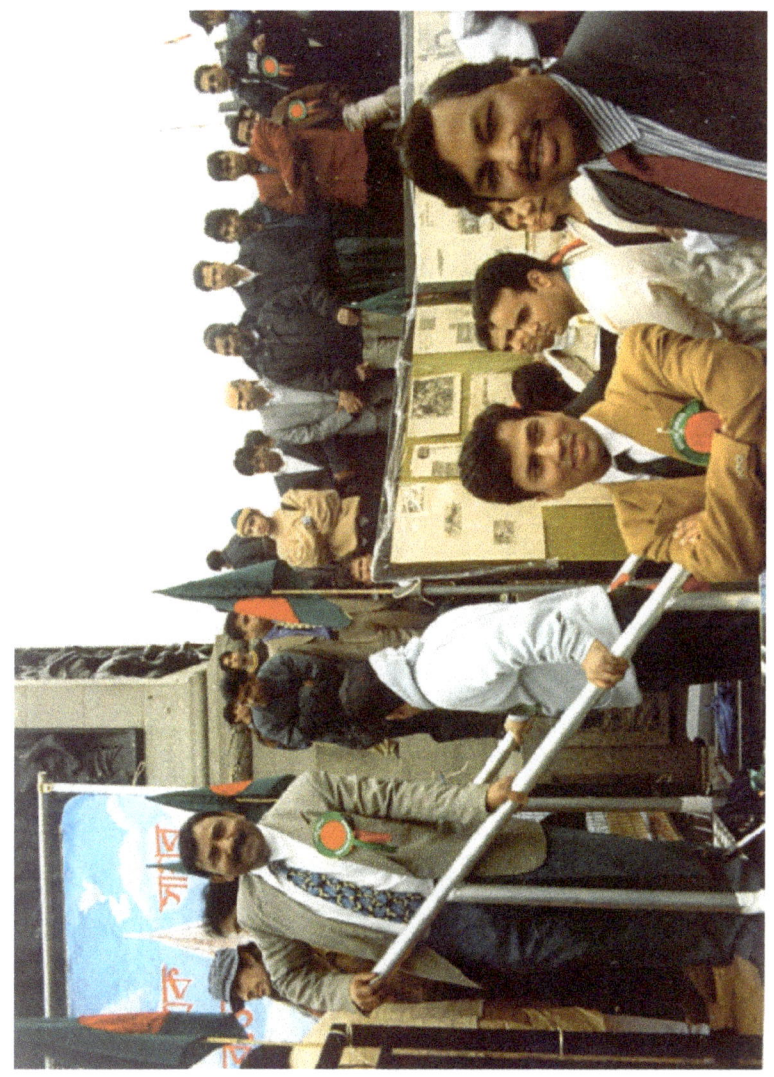

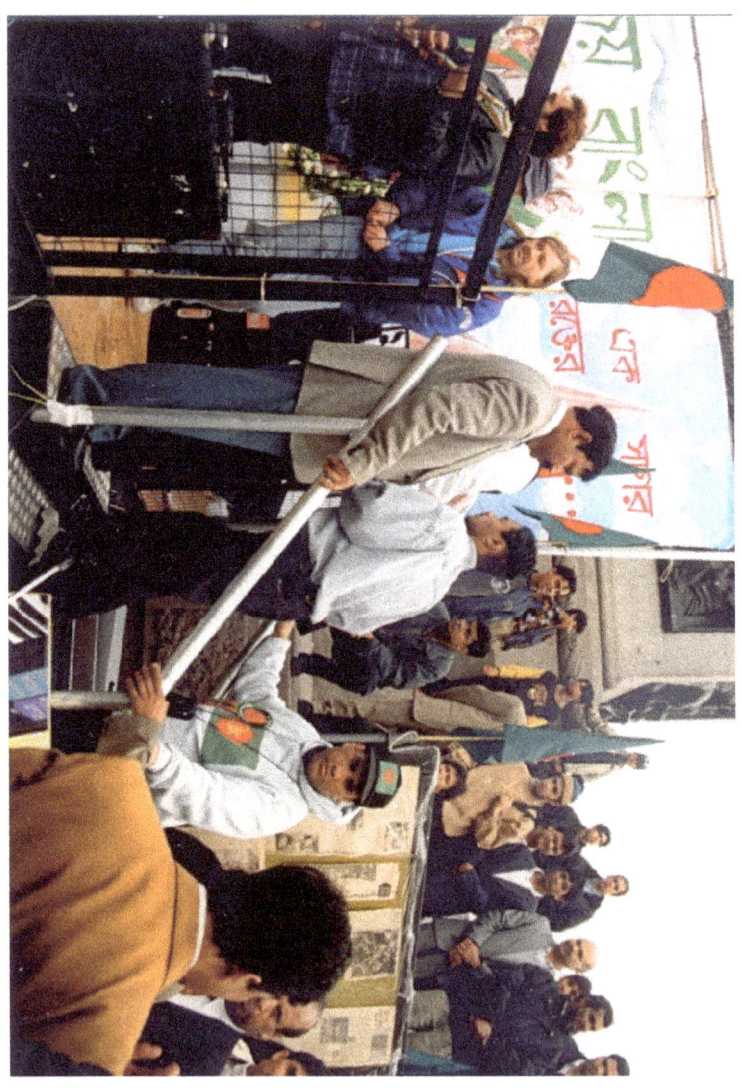

25th Anniversary of Bangladesh in Trafalgar Squares

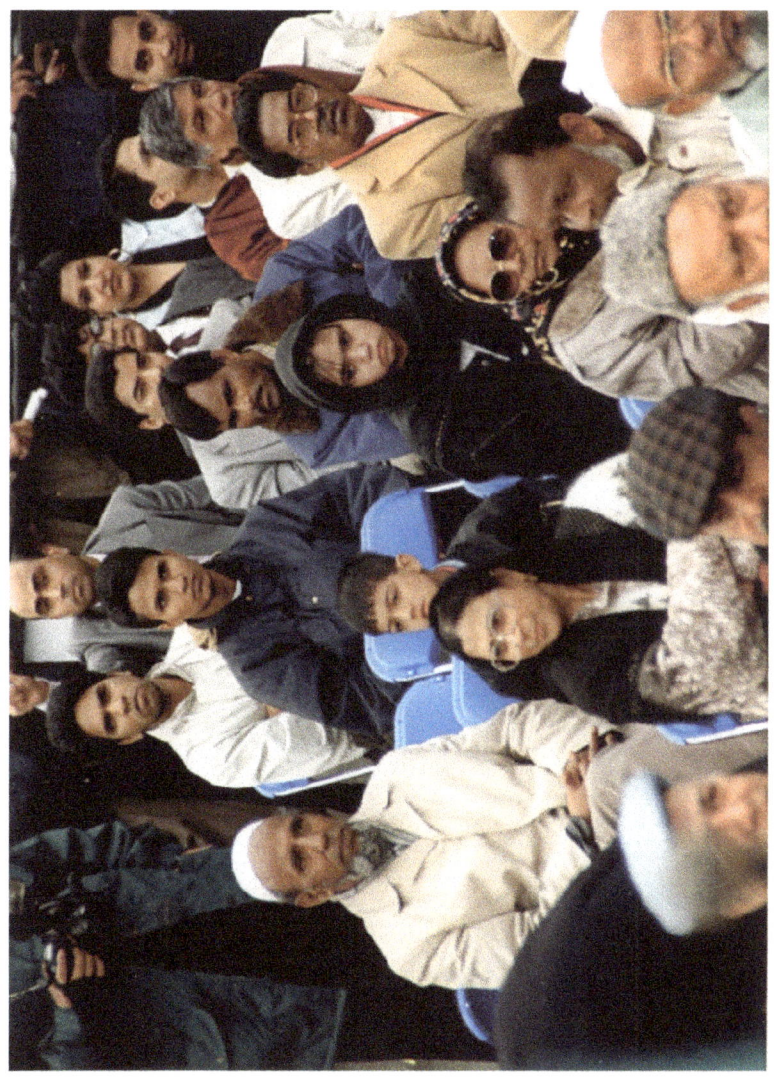

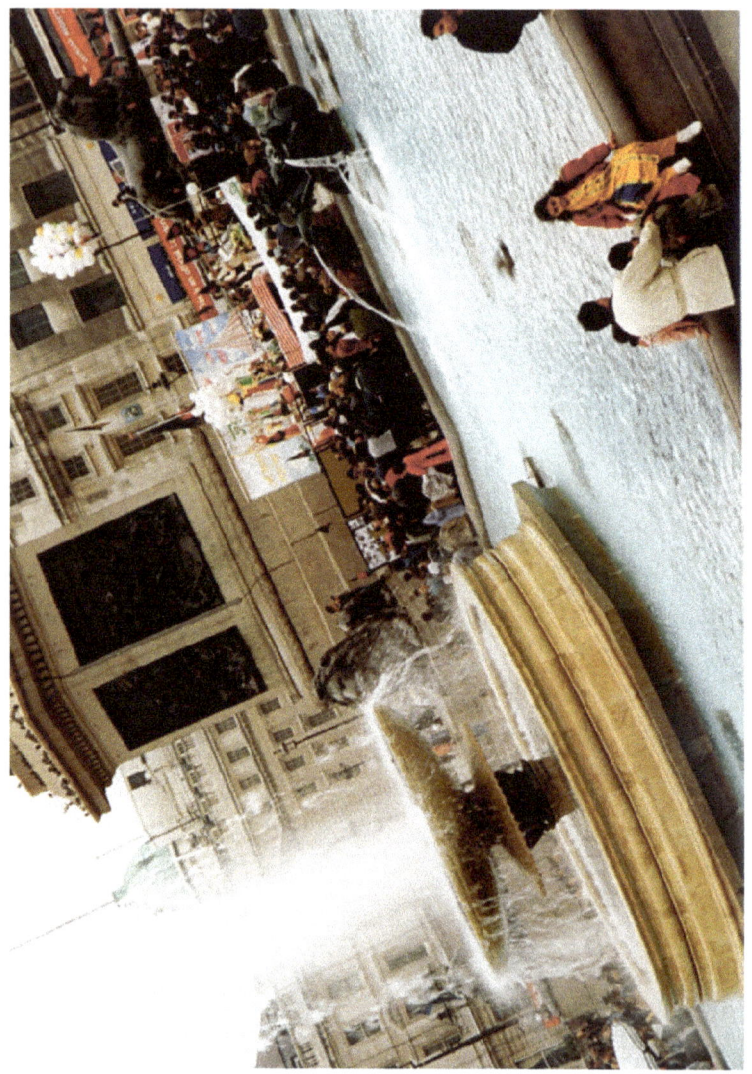

25th Anniversary of Bangladesh in Trafalgar Squares

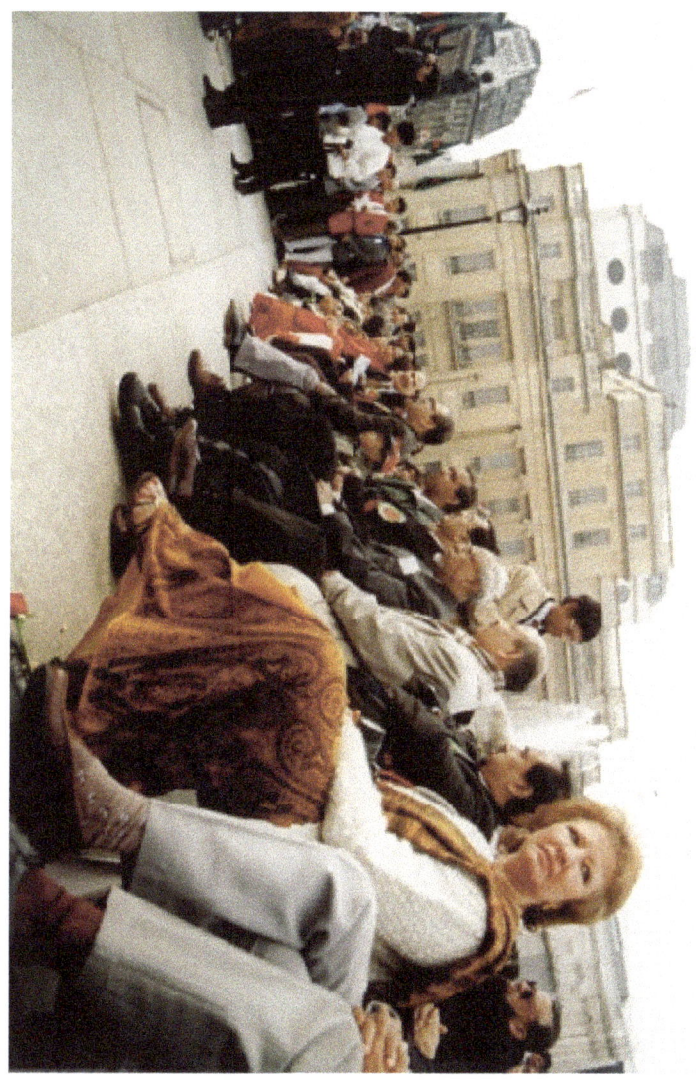

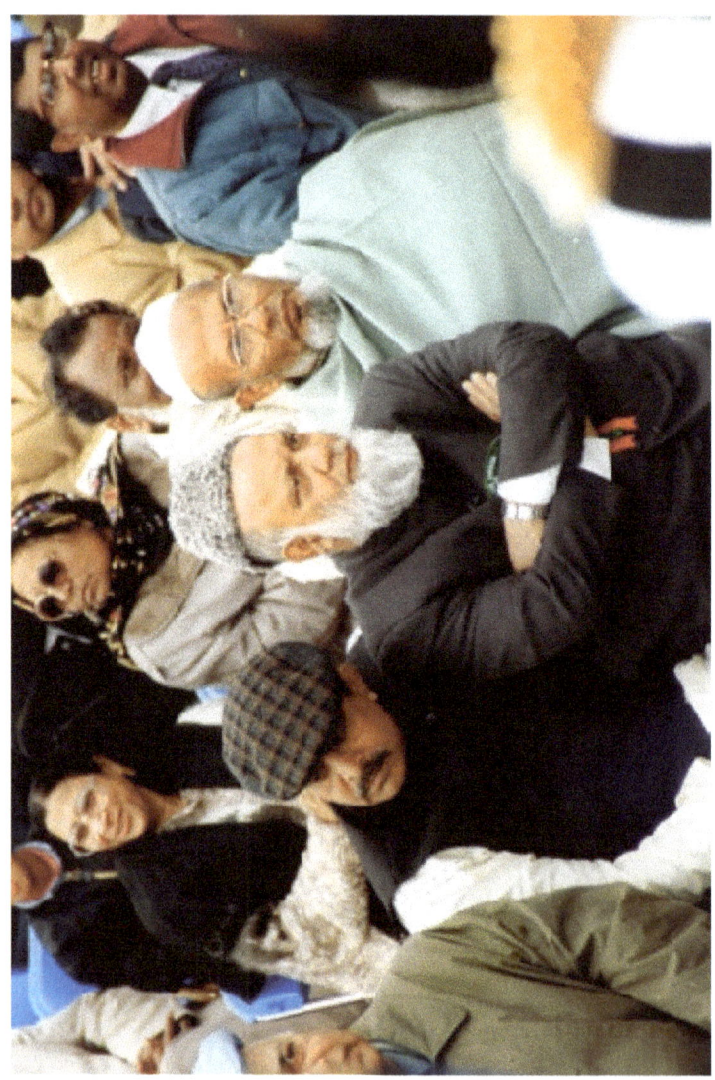

25th Anniversary of Bangladesh in Trafalgar Squares

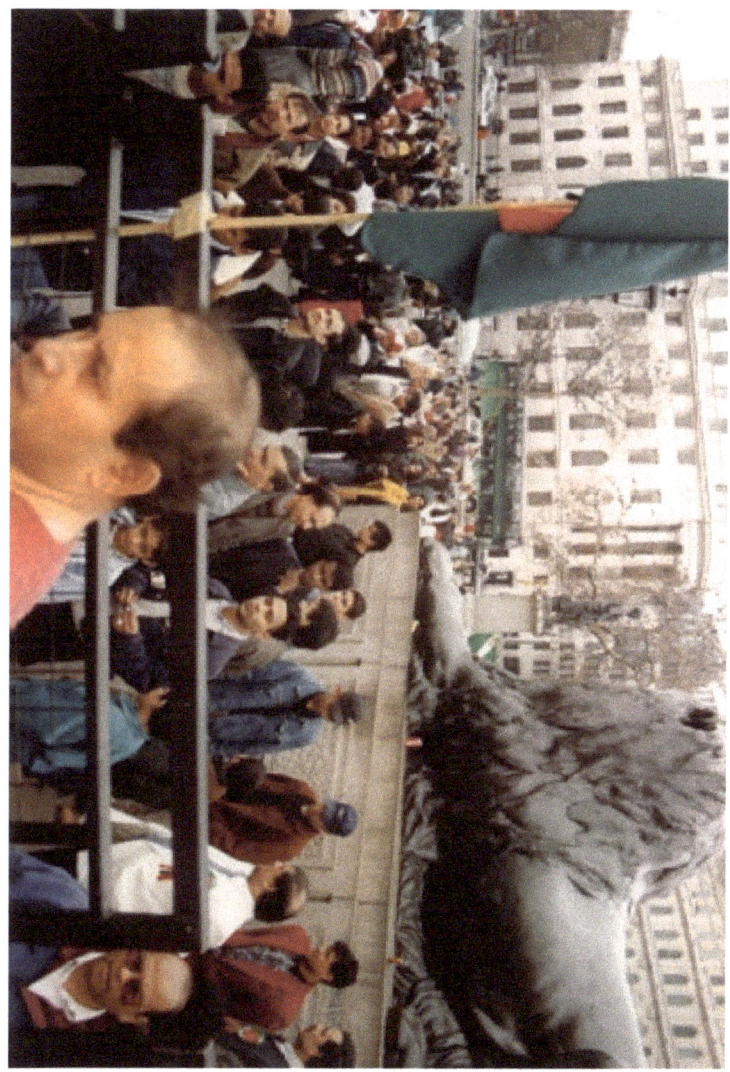

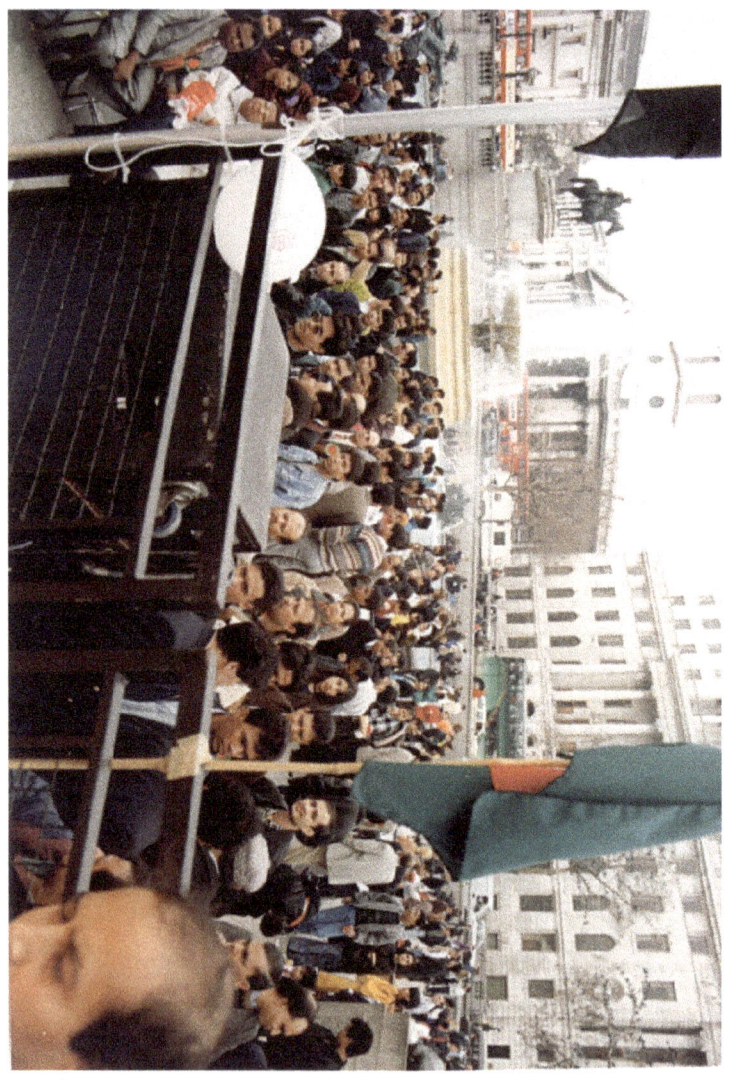

25th Anniversary of Bangladesh in Trafalgar Squares

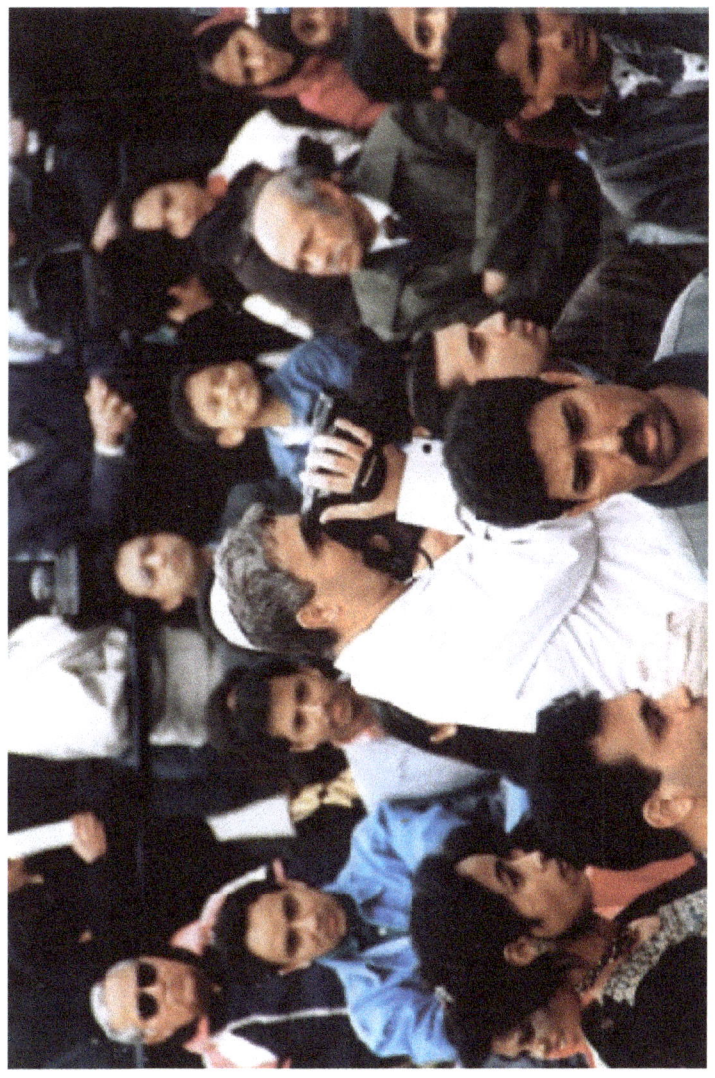

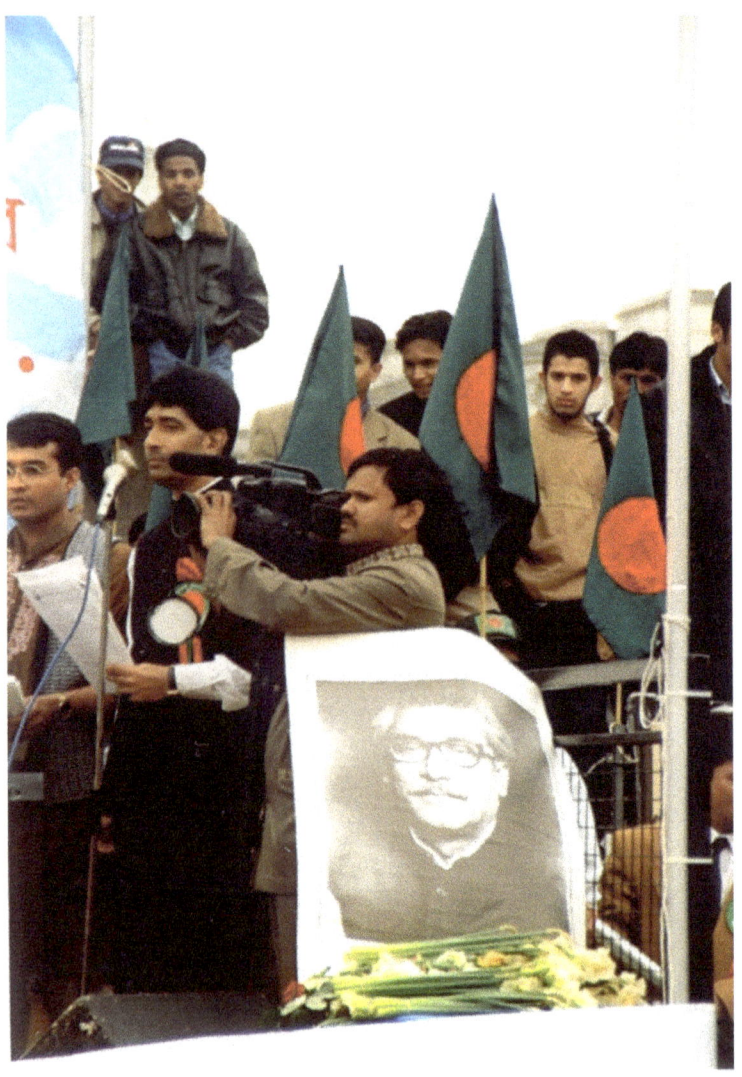

25th Anniversary of Bangladesh in Trafalgar Squares

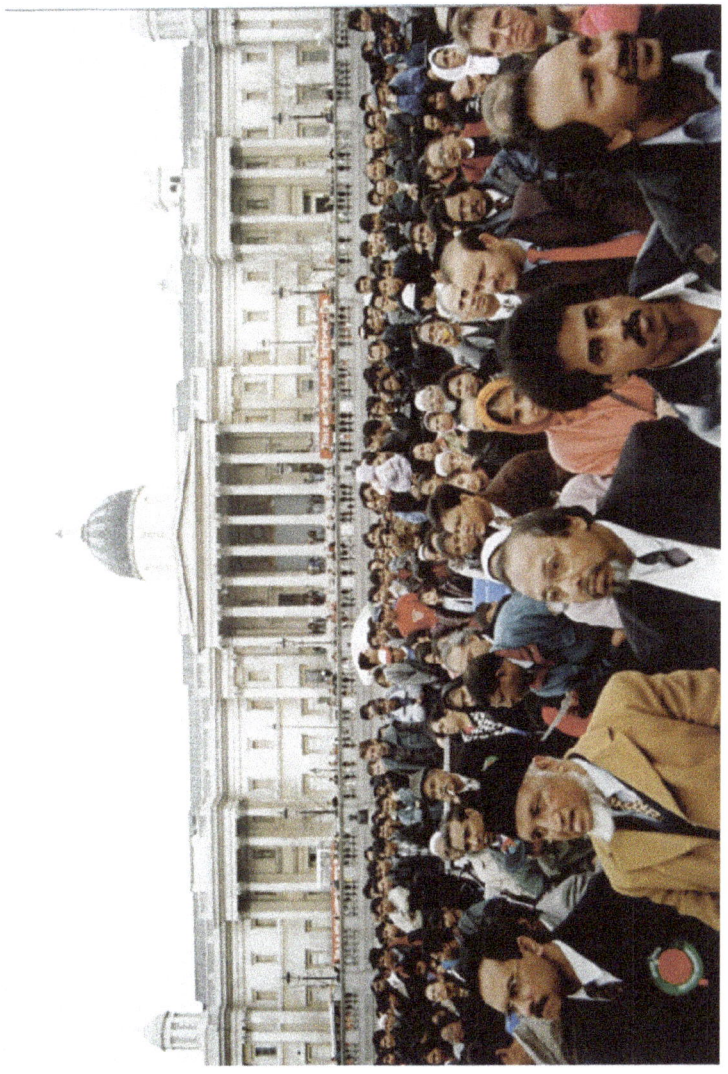

65

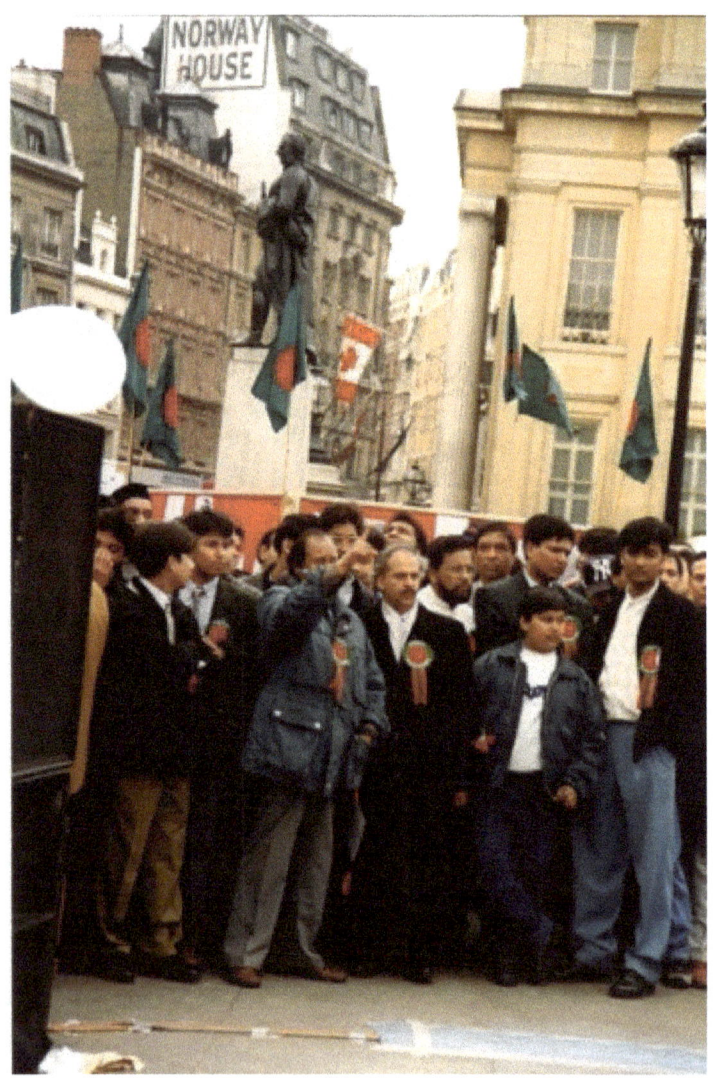

25th Anniversary of Bangladesh in Trafalgar Squares

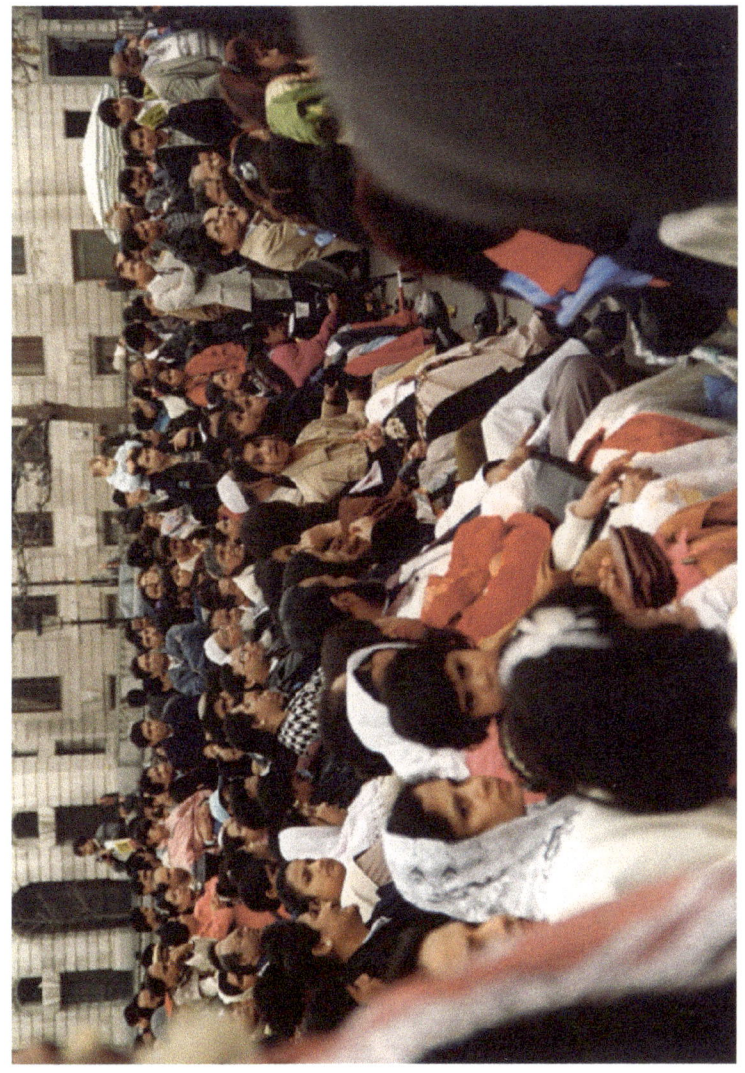

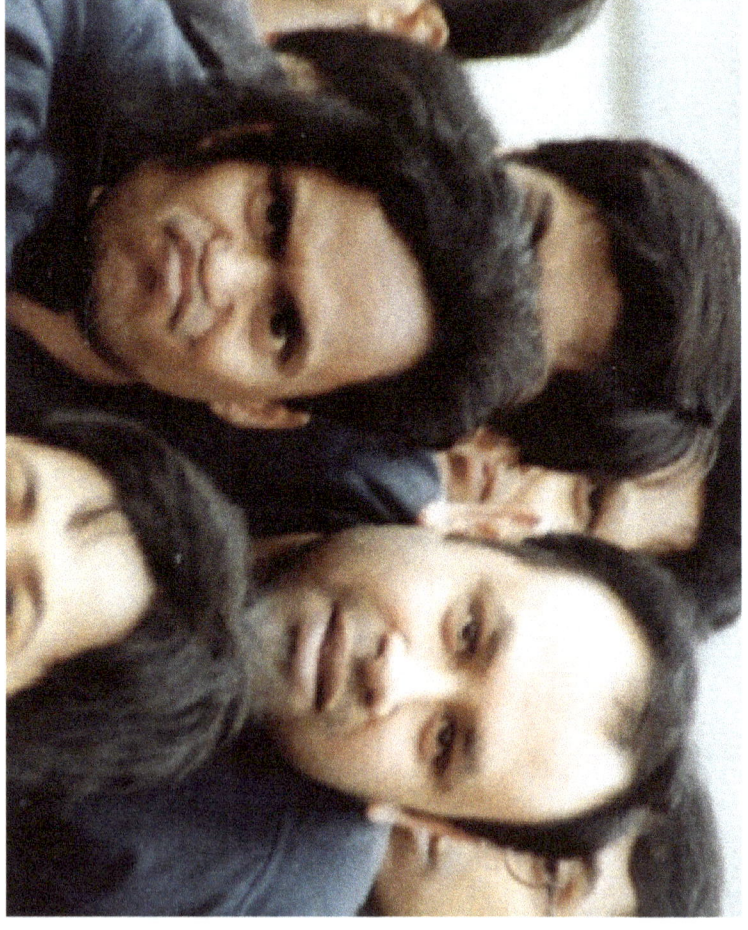

The artists and the white doves

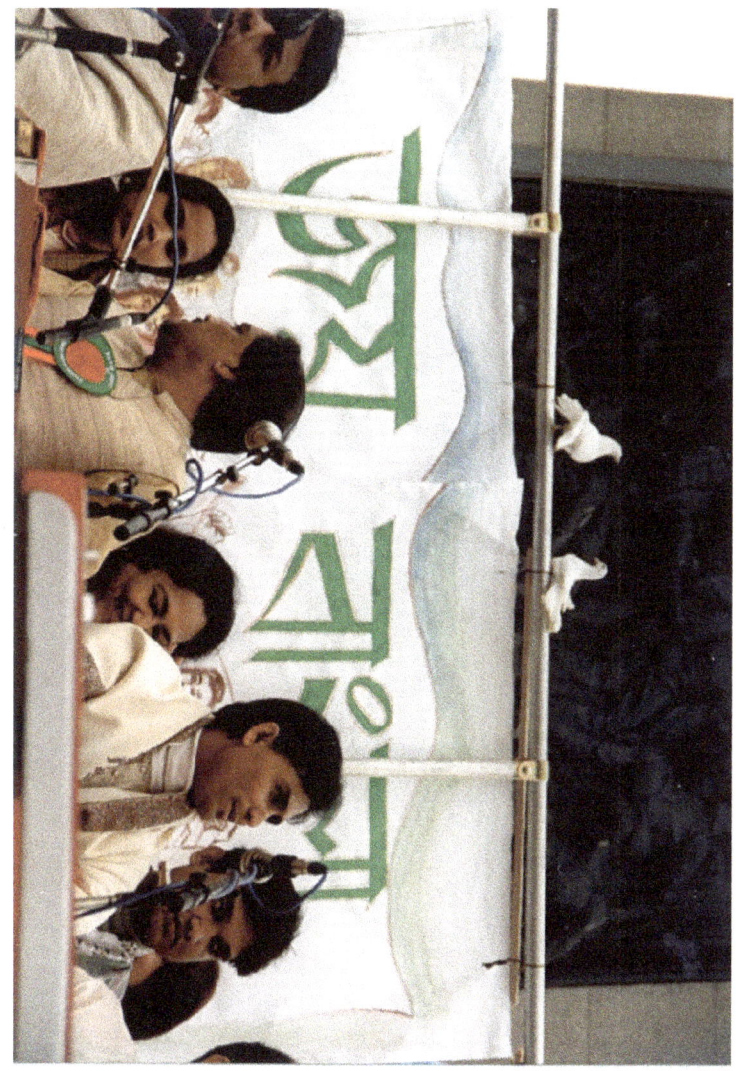

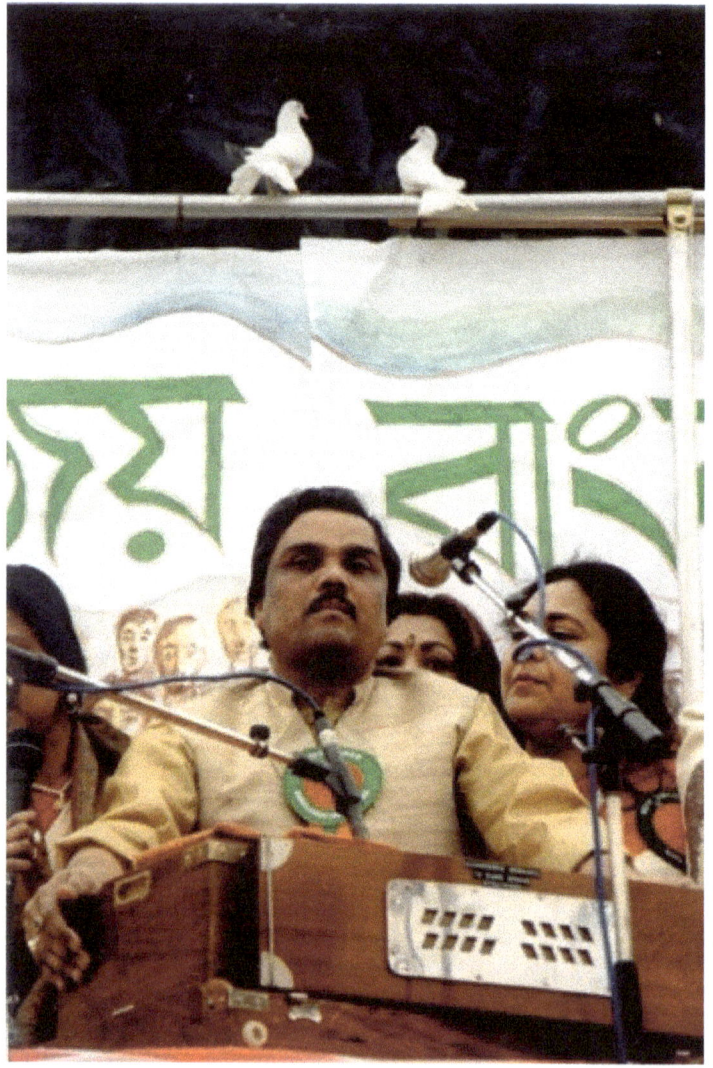

25th Anniversary of Bangladesh in Trafalgar Squares

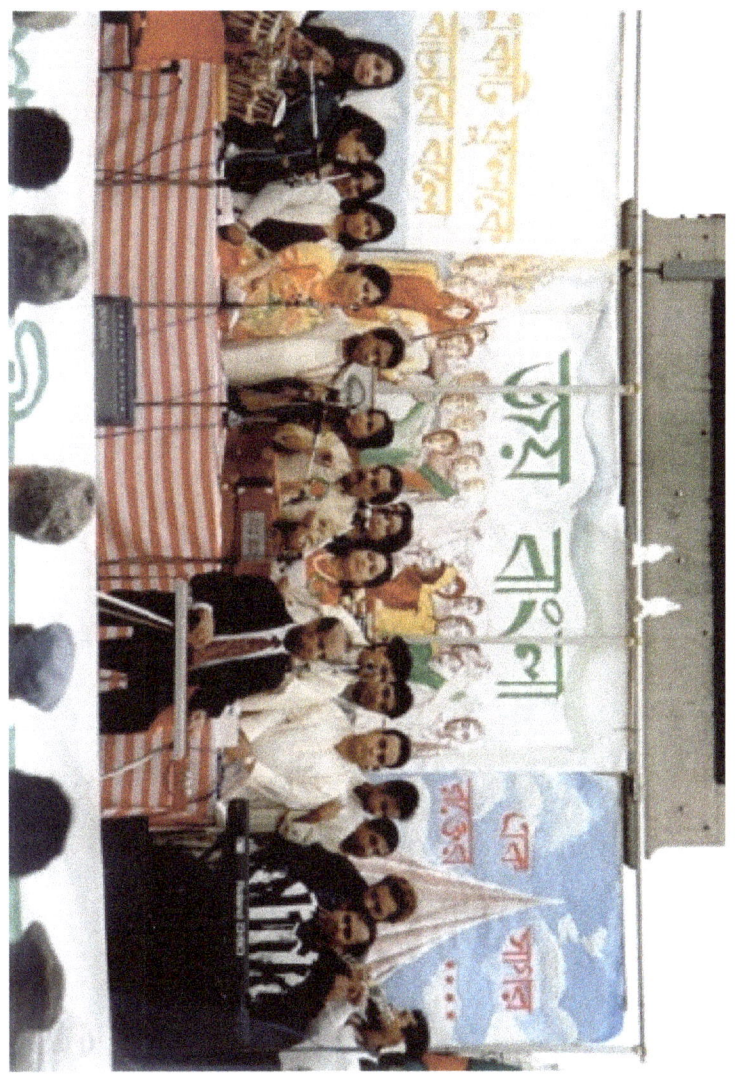

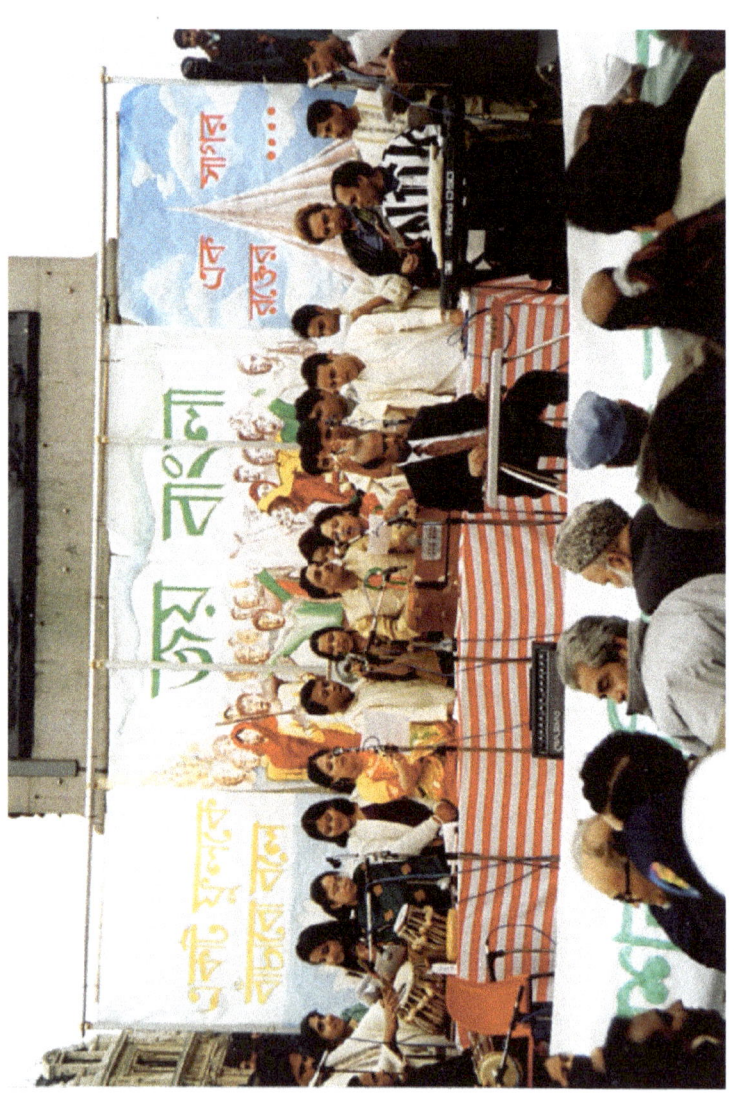

25th Anniversary of Bangladesh in Trafalgar Squares

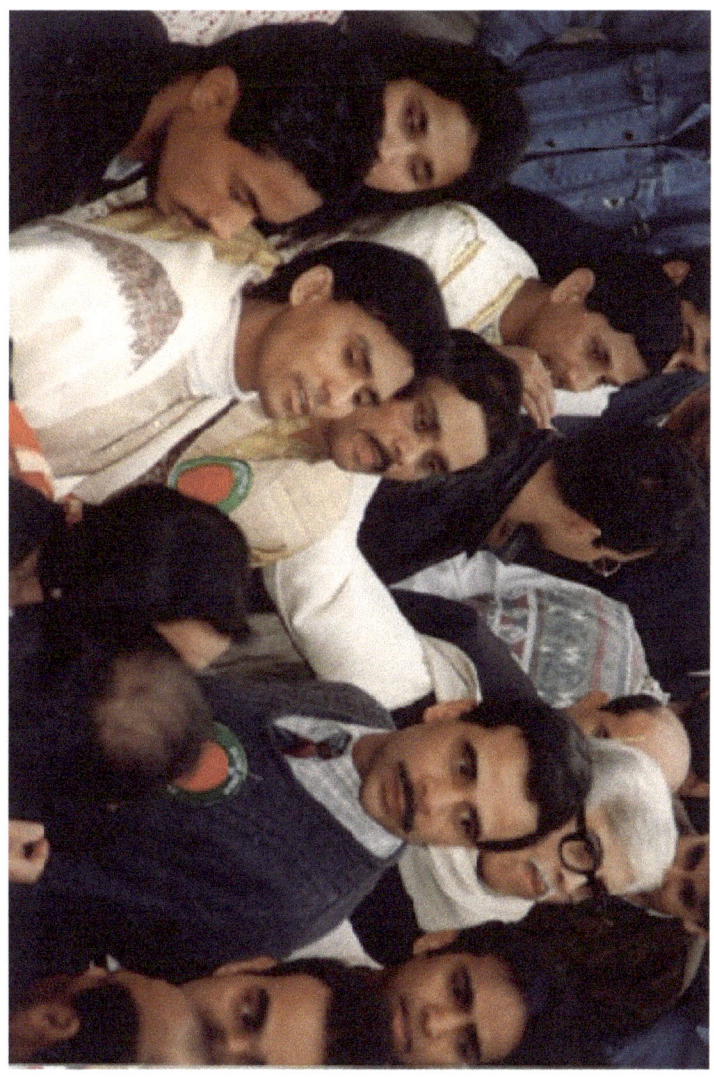

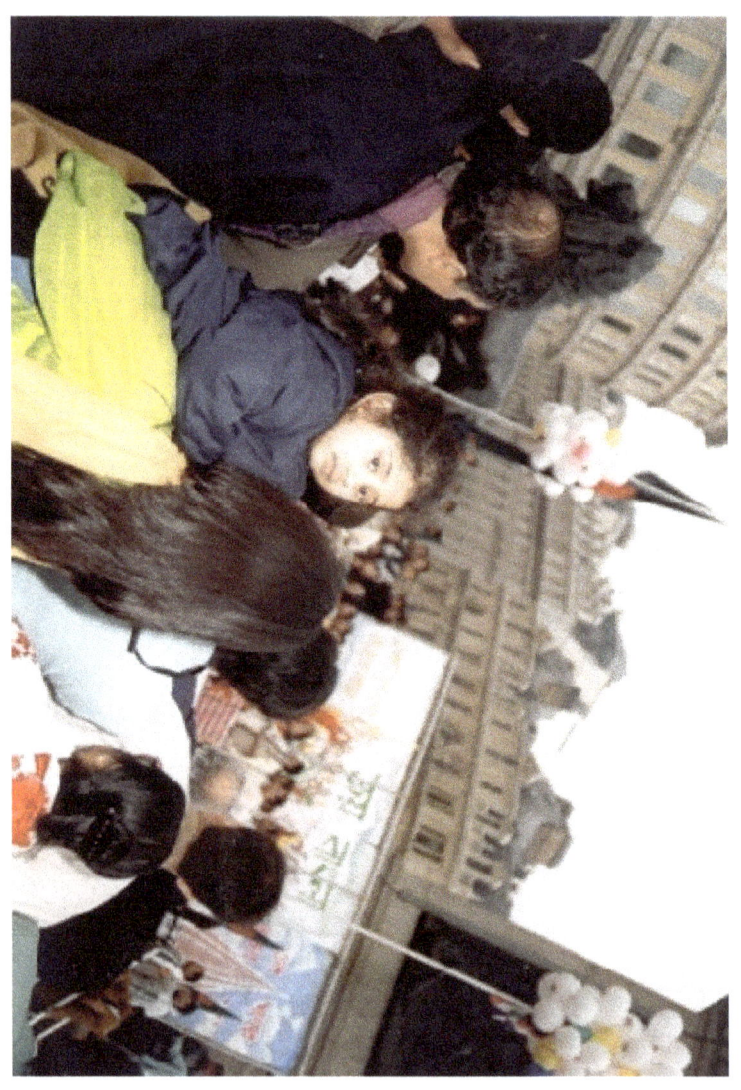

25th Anniversary of Bangladesh in Trafalgar Squares

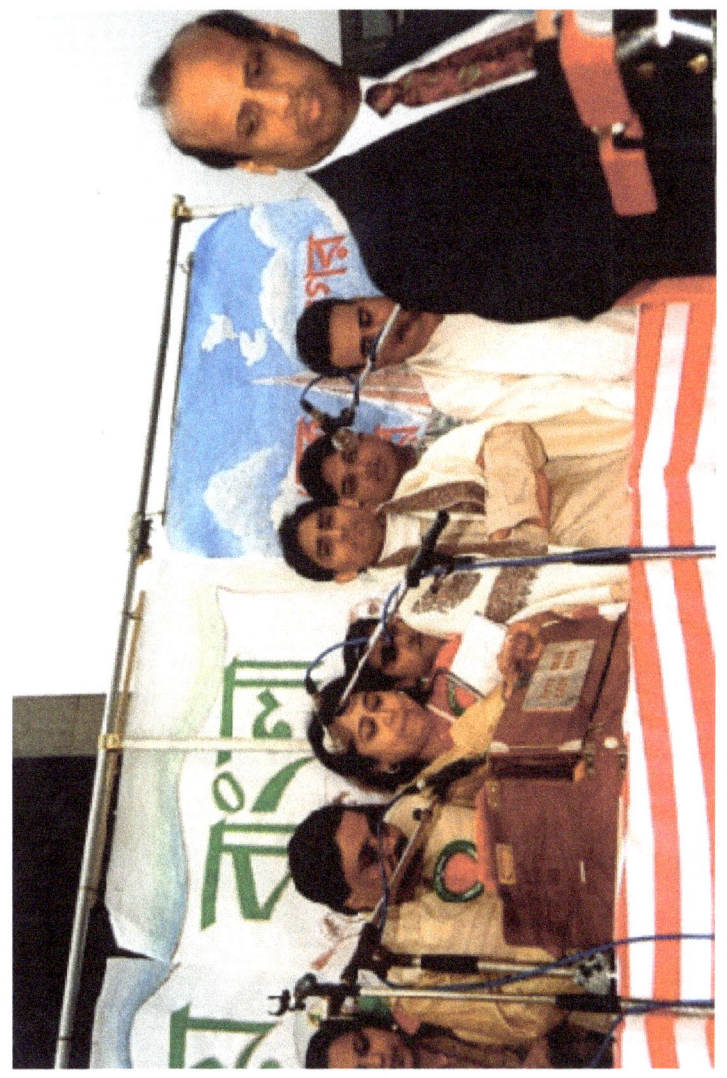

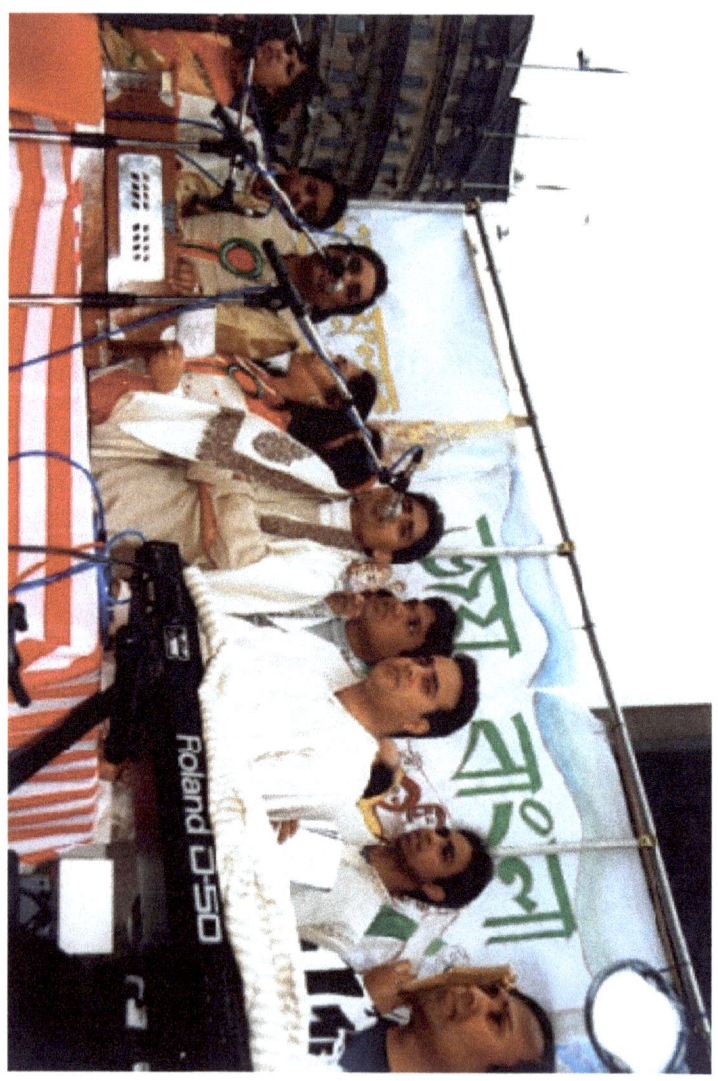

25th Anniversary of Bangladesh in Trafalgar Squares

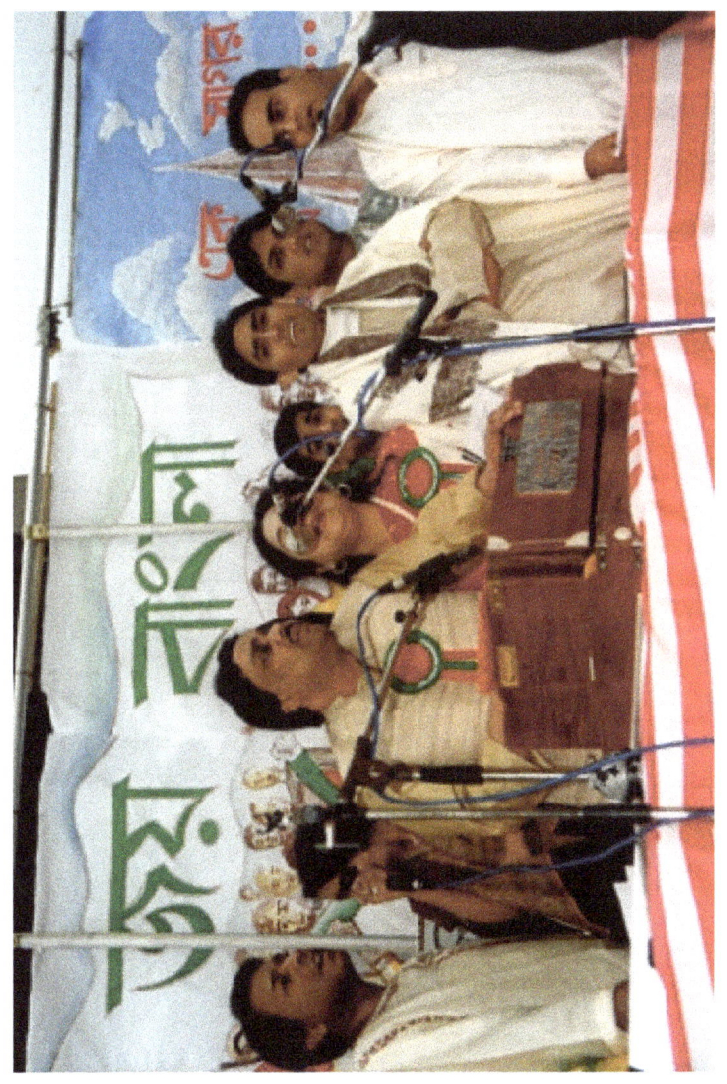

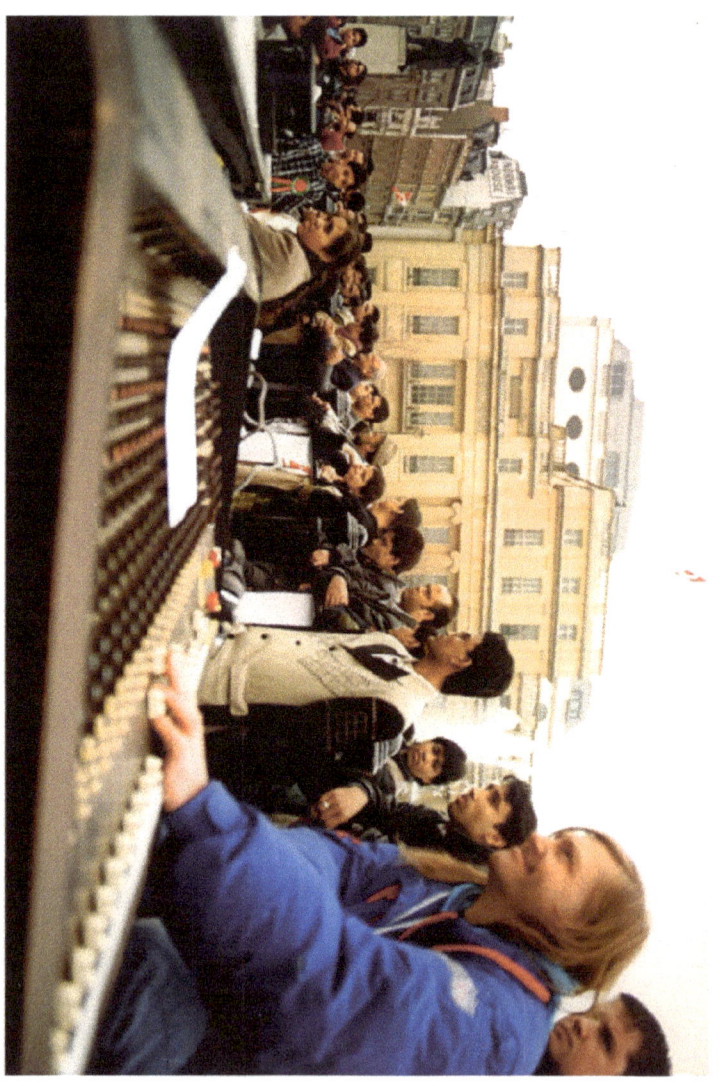

25th Anniversary of Bangladesh in Trafalgar Squares

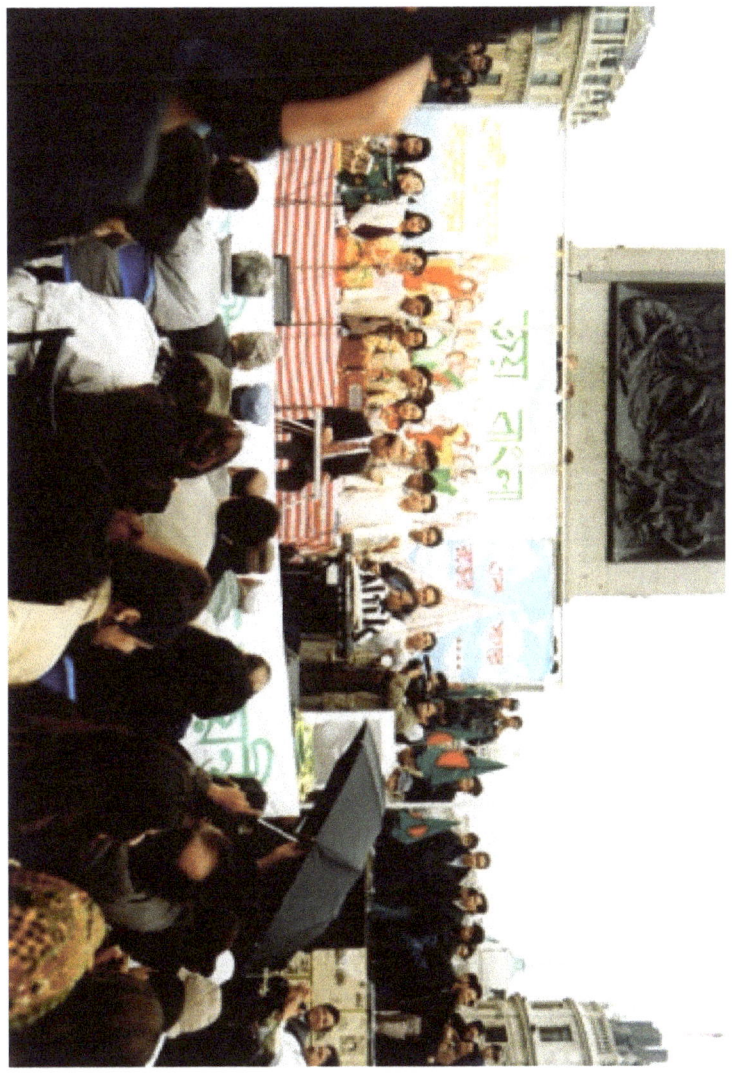

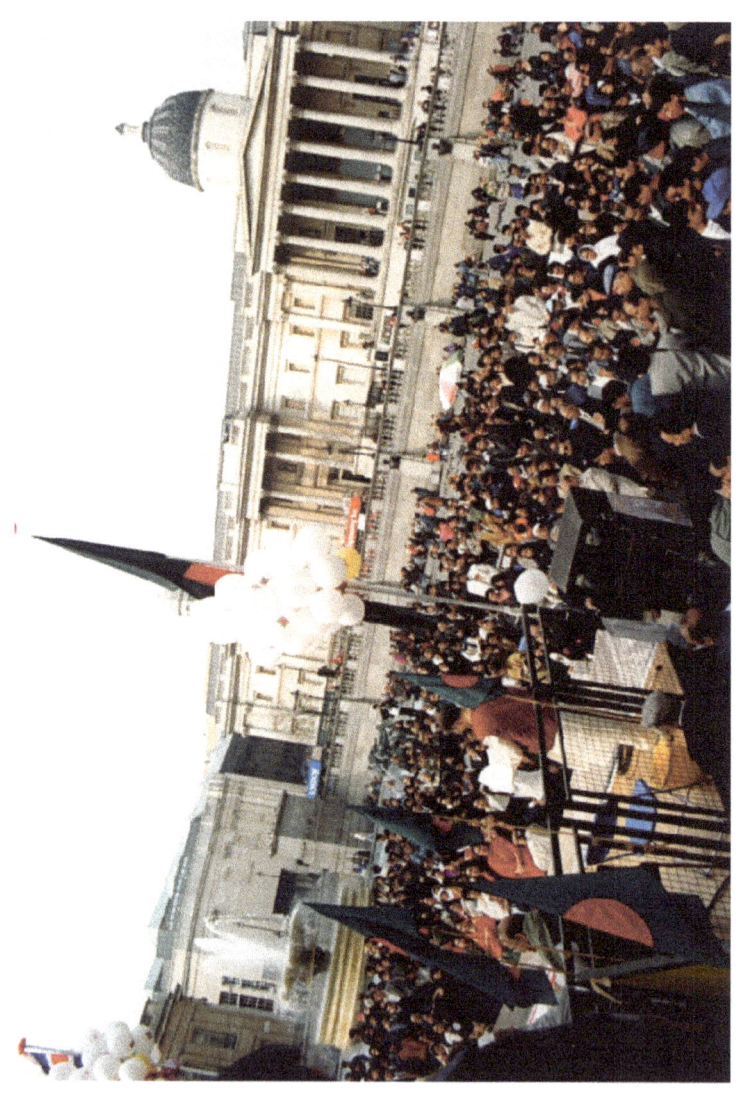

25th Anniversary of Bangladesh in Trafalgar Squares

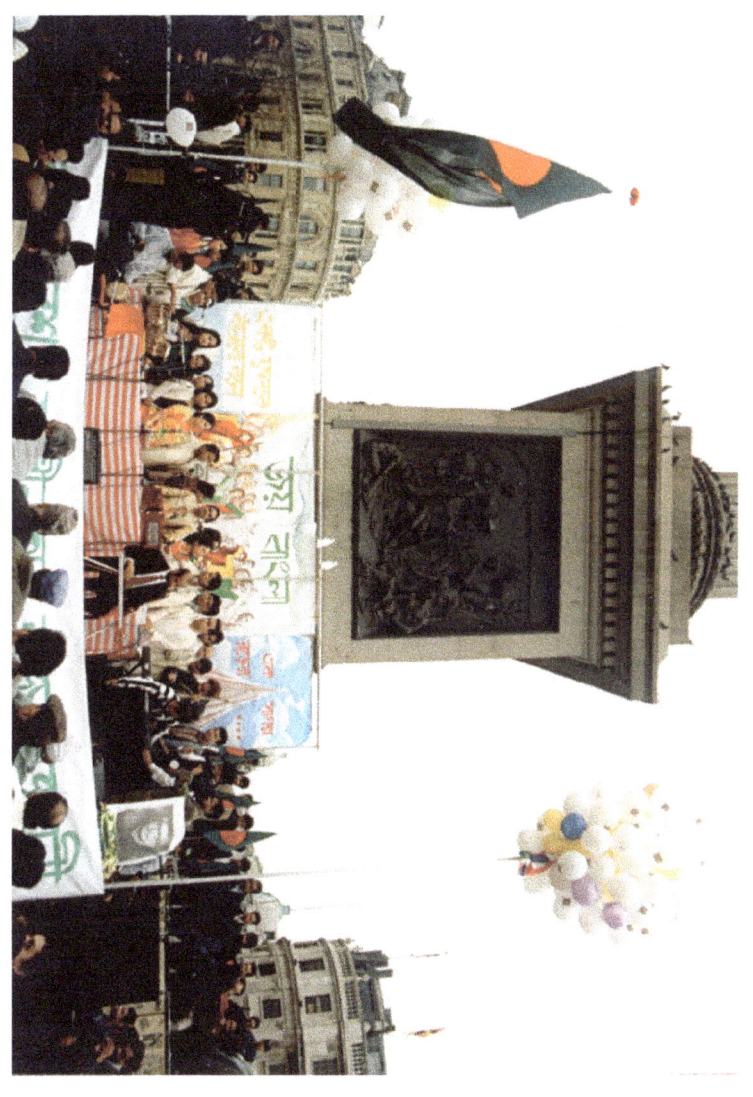

The Jubilation

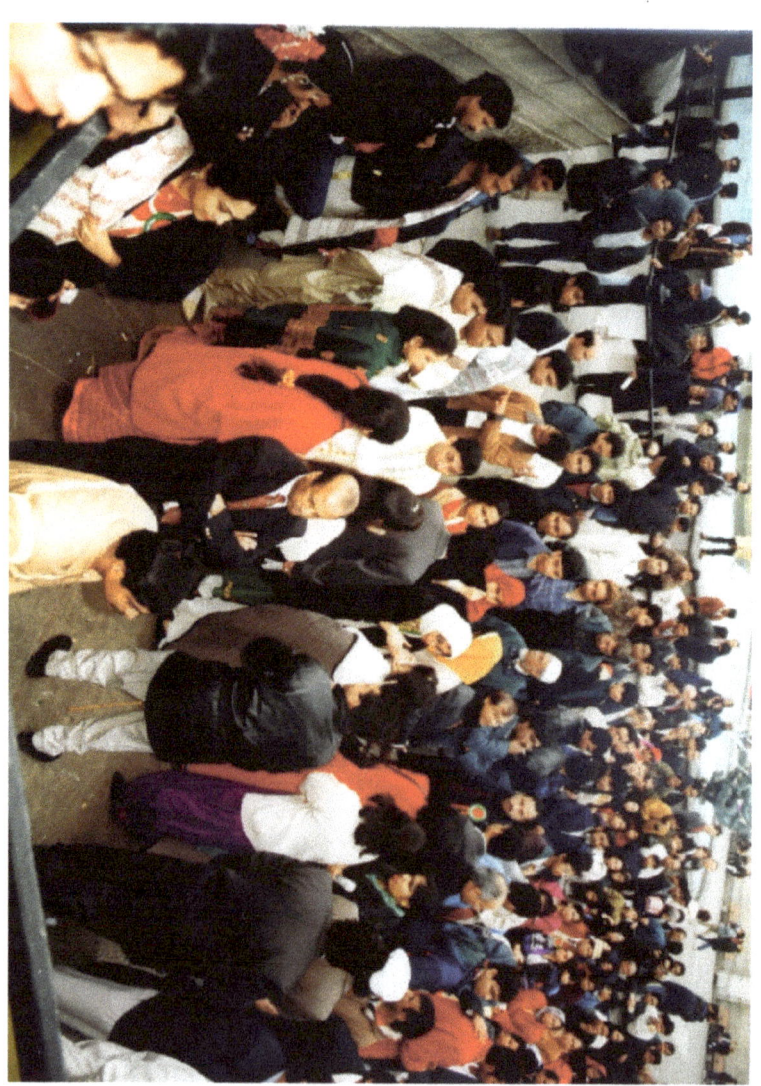

25th Anniversary of Bangladesh in Trafalgar Squares

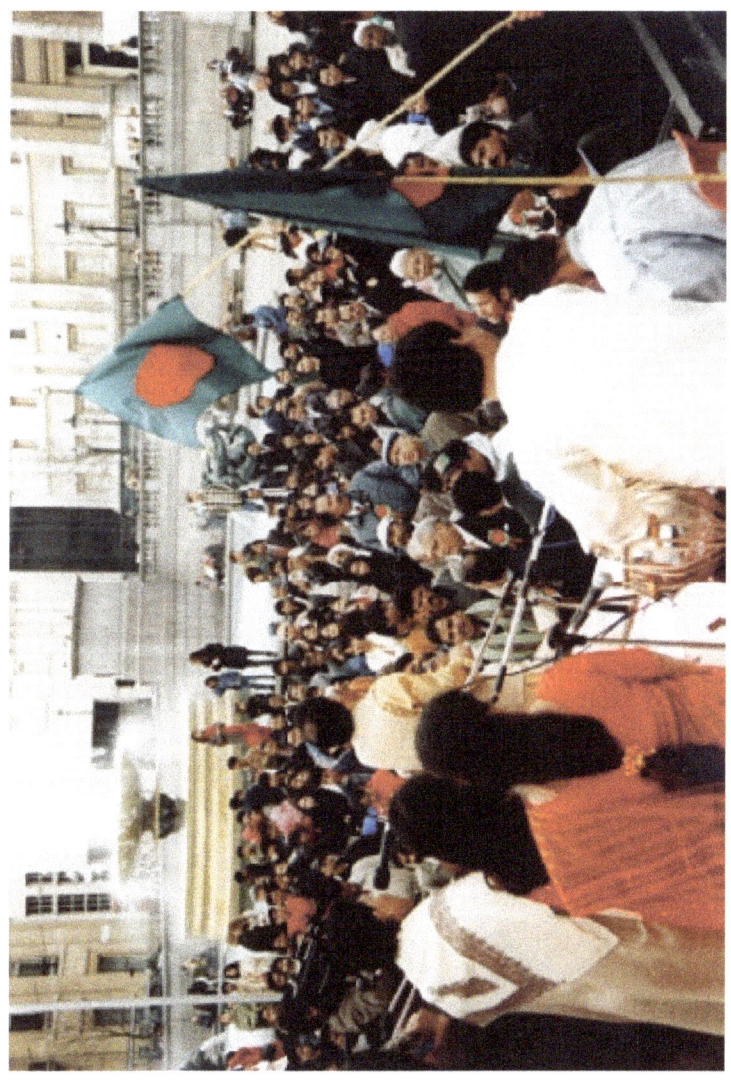

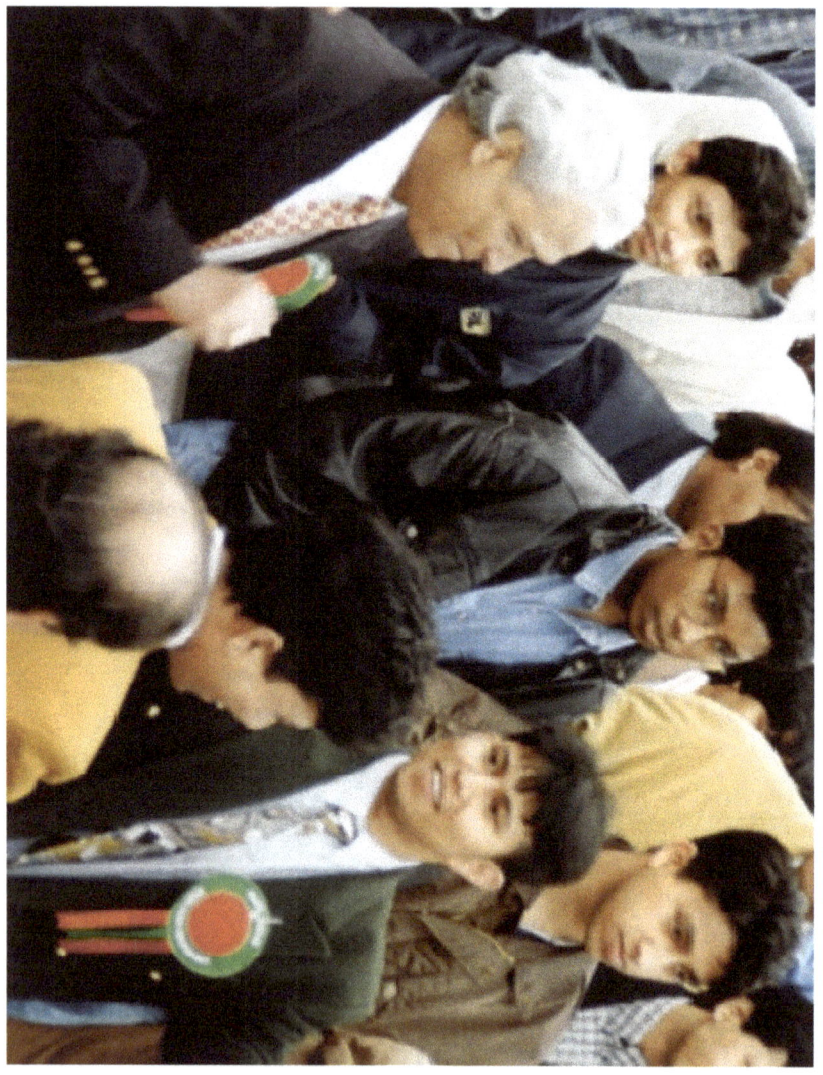

25th Anniversary of Bangladesh in Trafalgar Squares

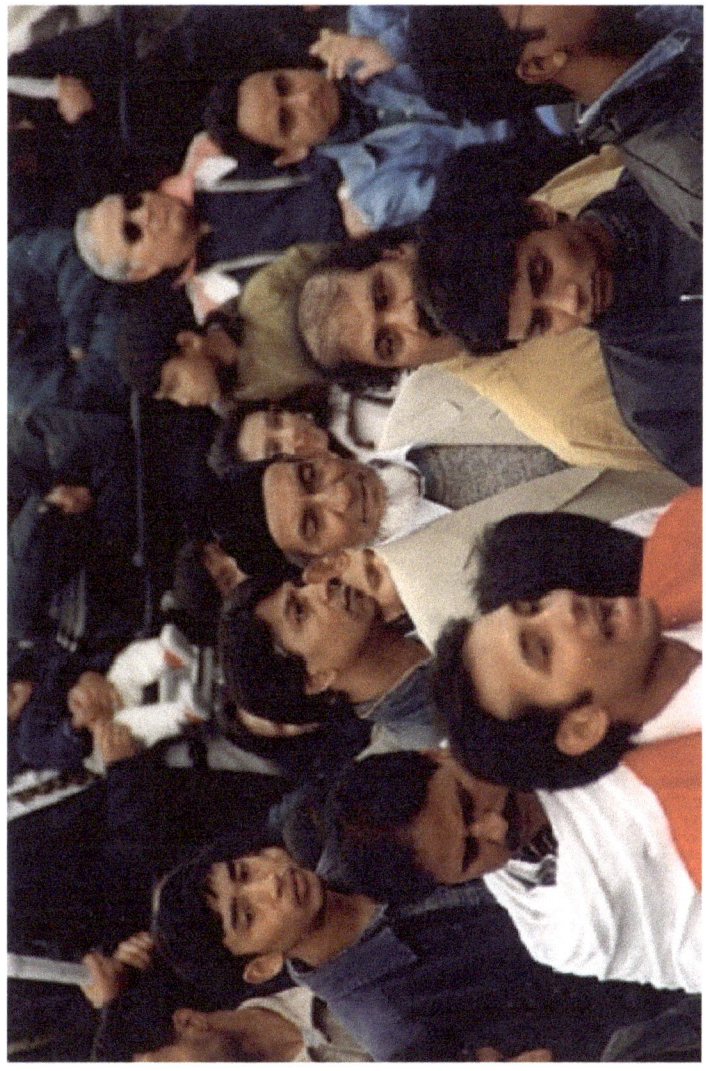

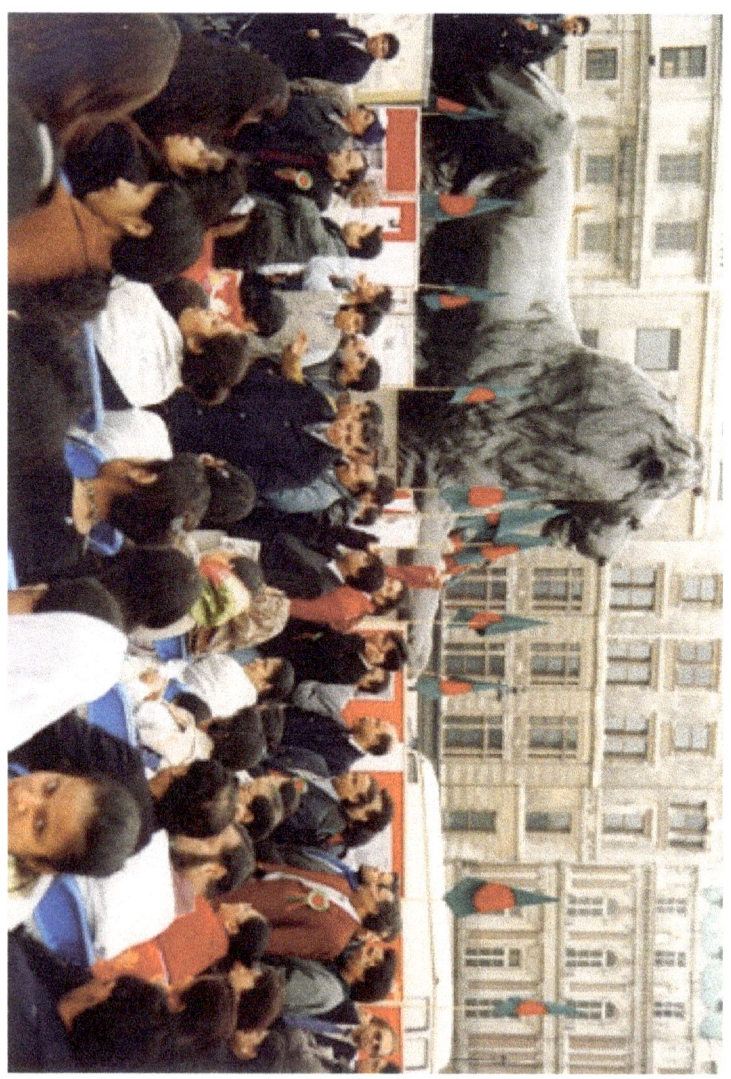

25th Anniversary of Bangladesh in Trafalgar Squares

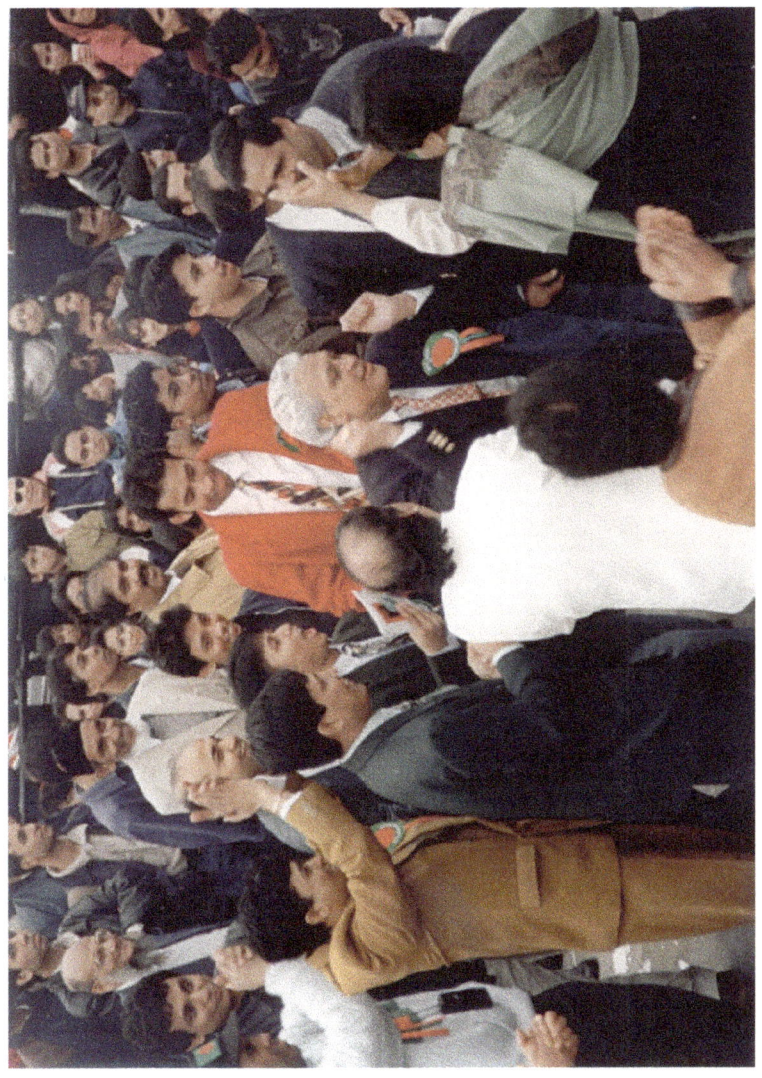

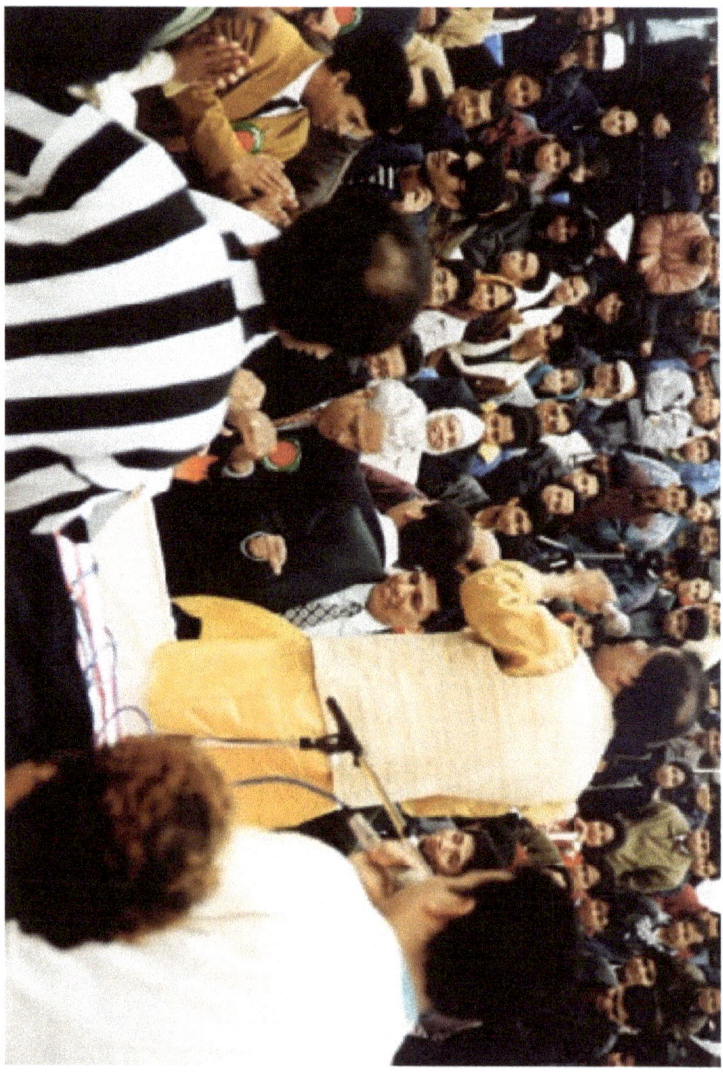

25th Anniversary of Bangladesh in Trafalgar Squares

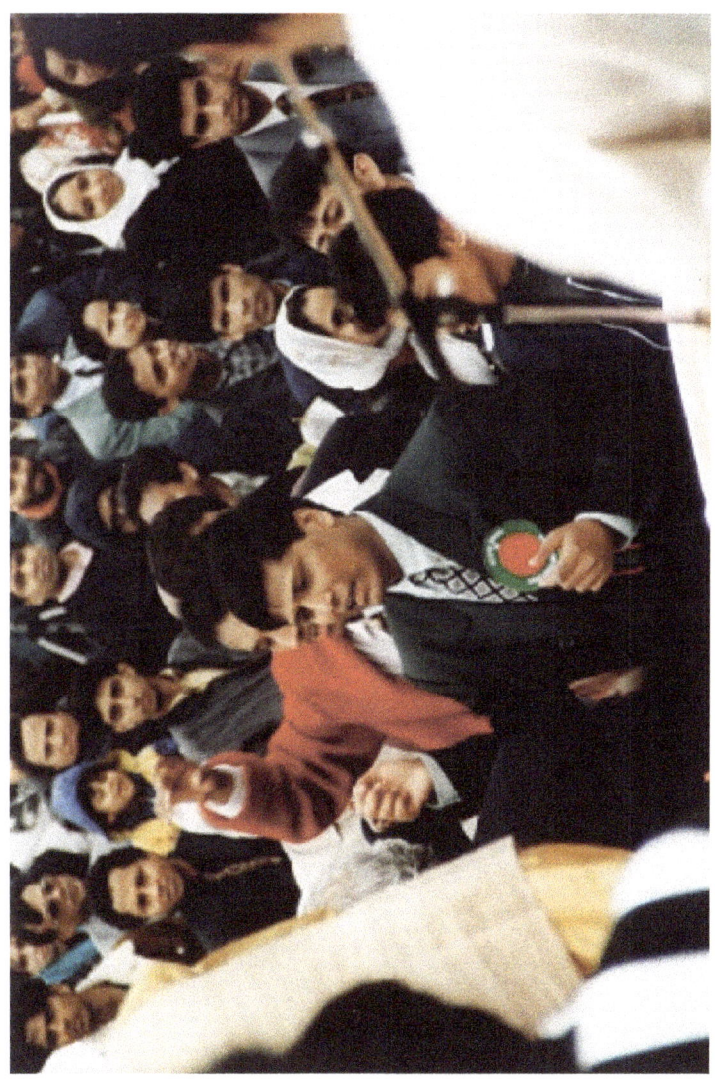

89

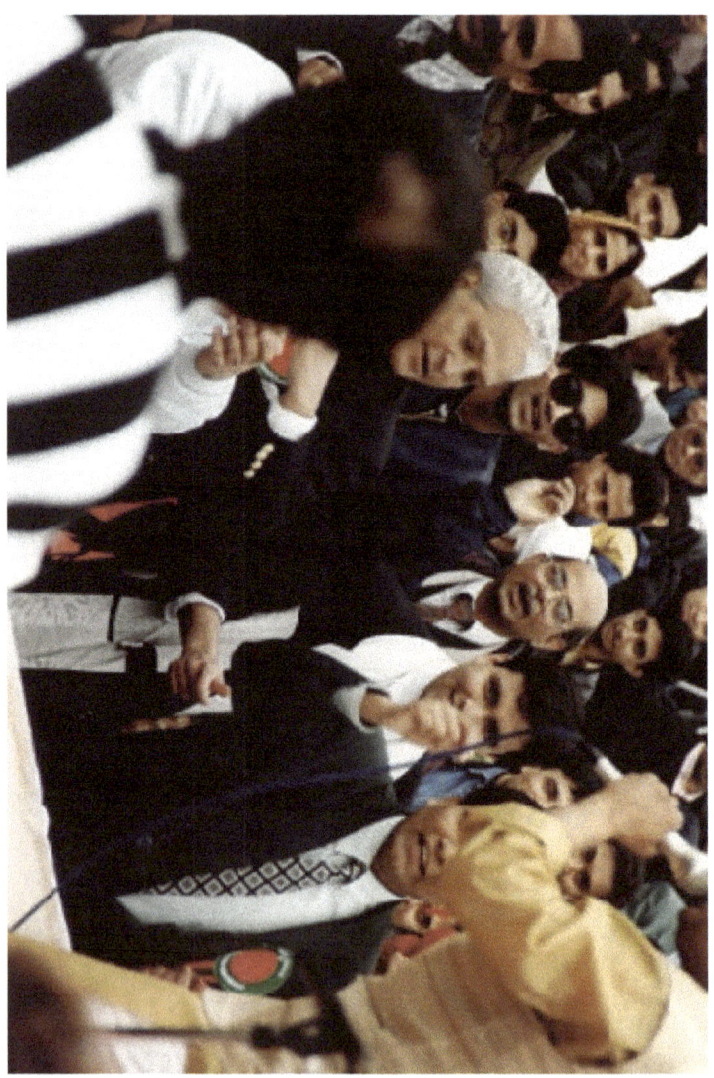

25th Anniversary of Bangladesh in Trafalgar Squares

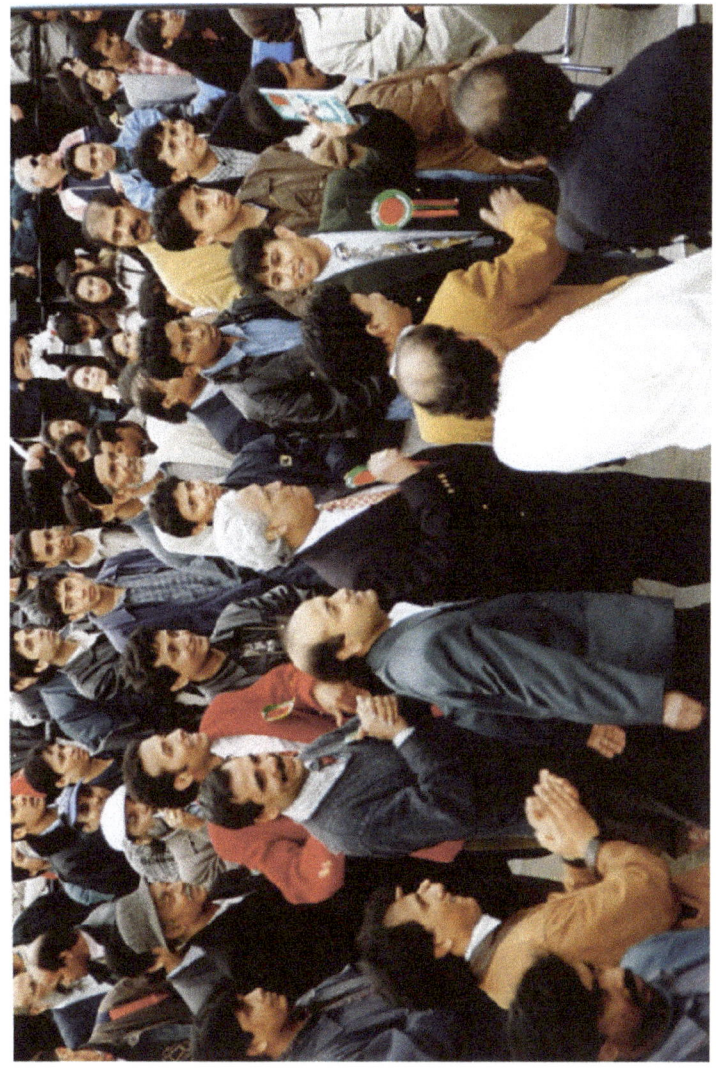

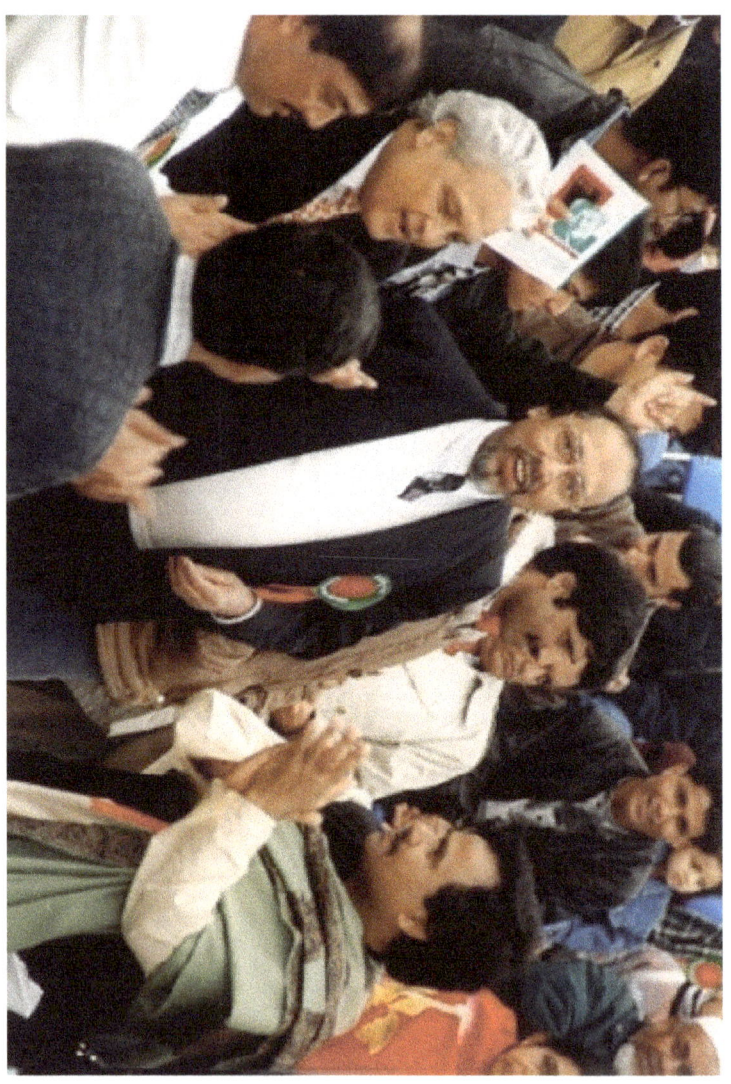

25th Anniversary of Bangladesh in Trafalgar Squares

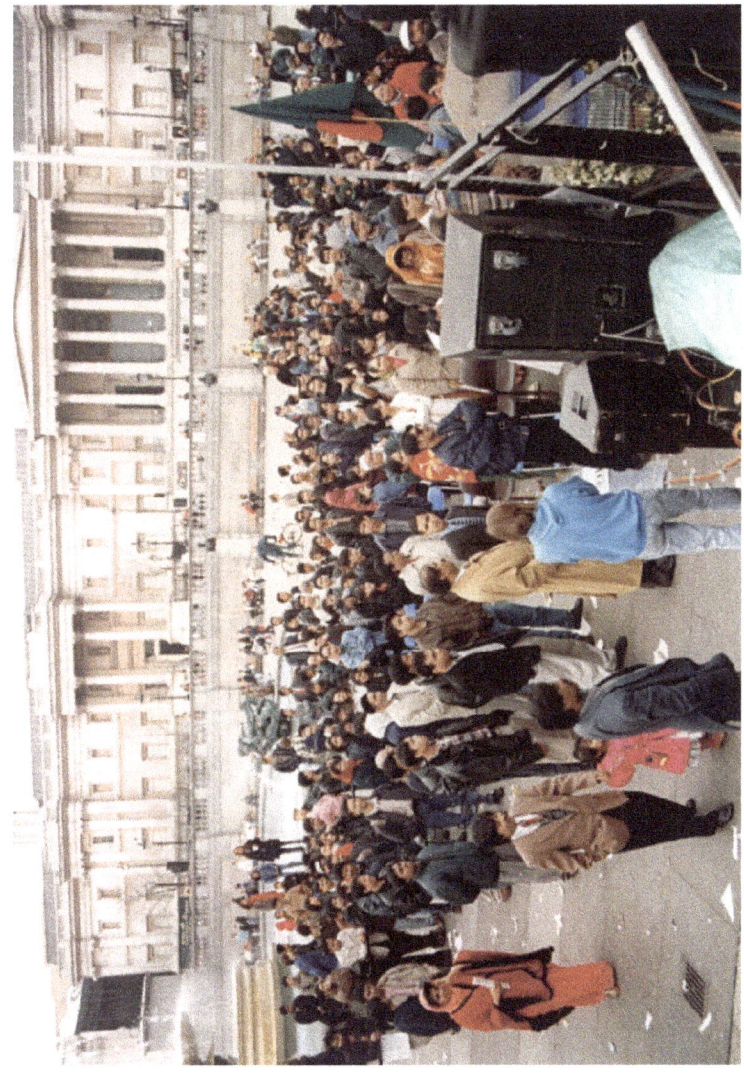

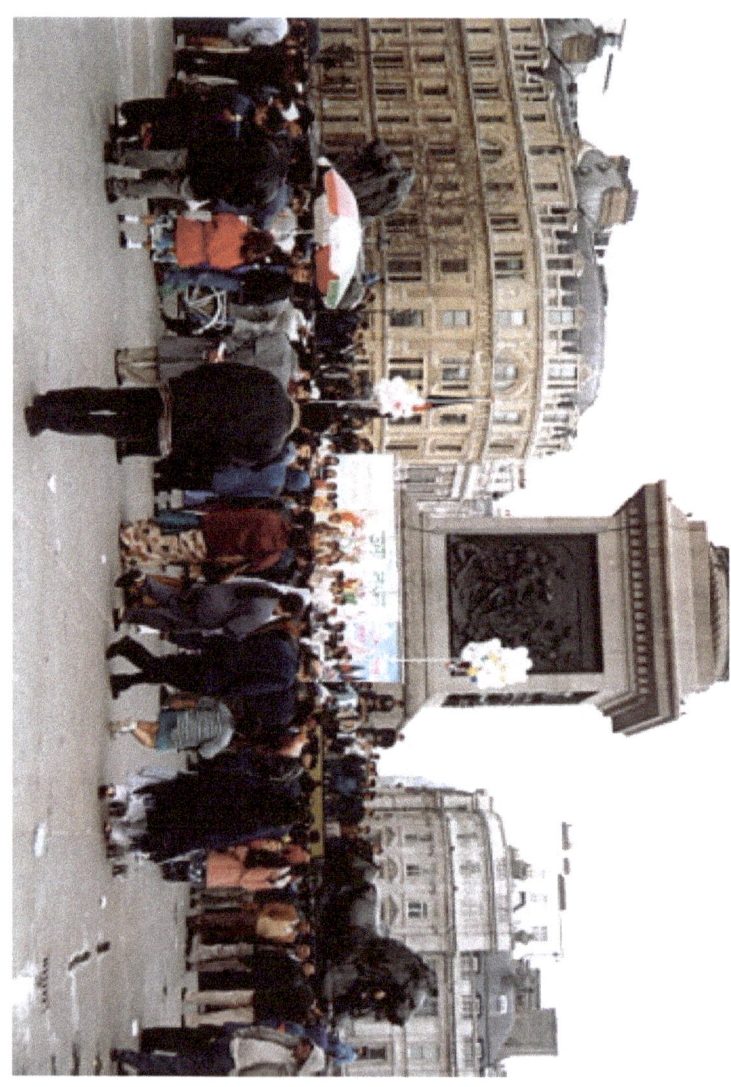

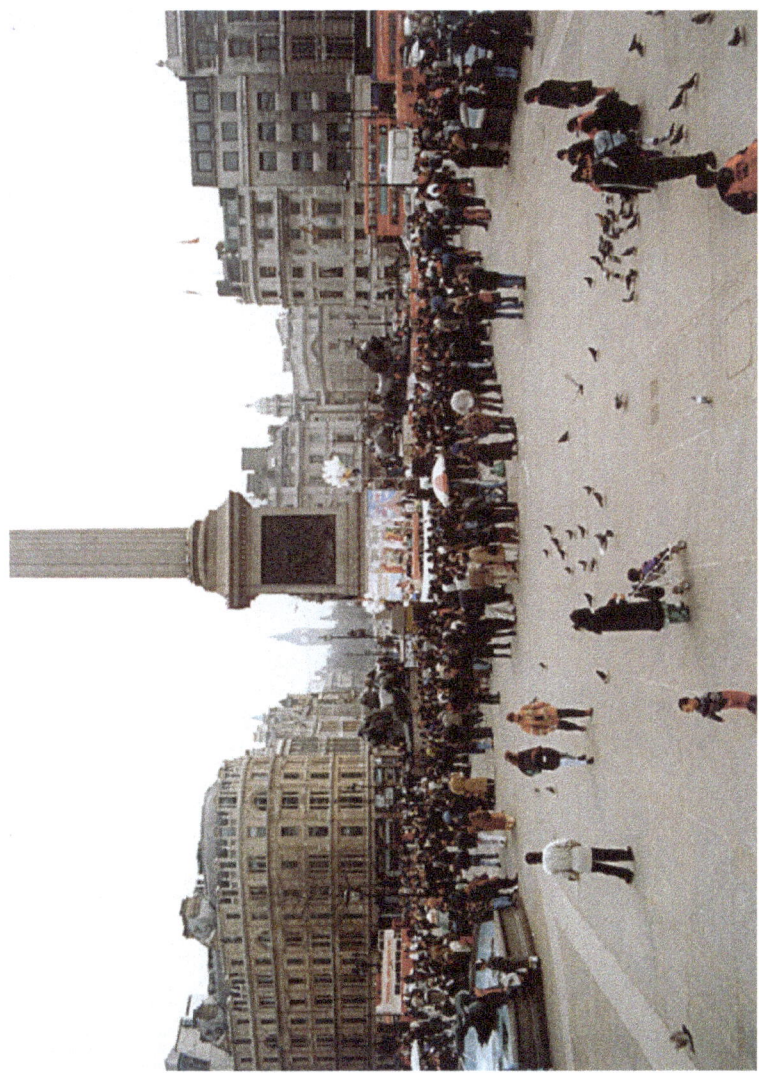

Pigeons were around then.

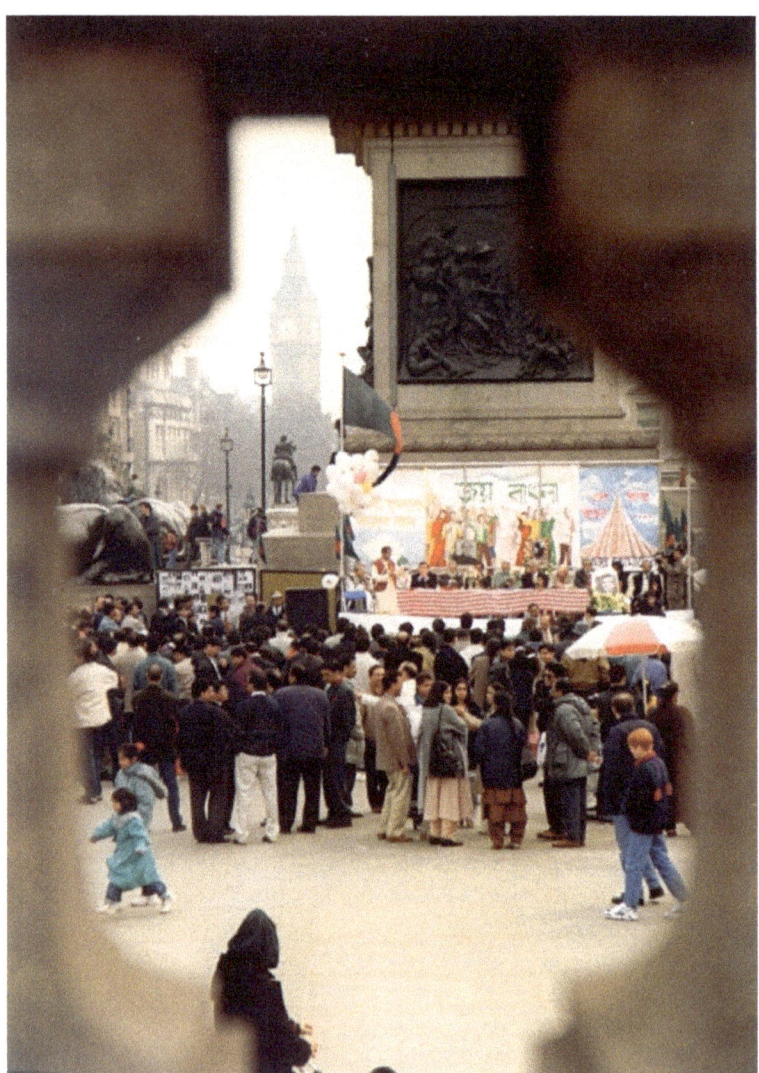
Child's eye view of the event.

25th Anniversary of Bangladesh in Trafalgar Squares

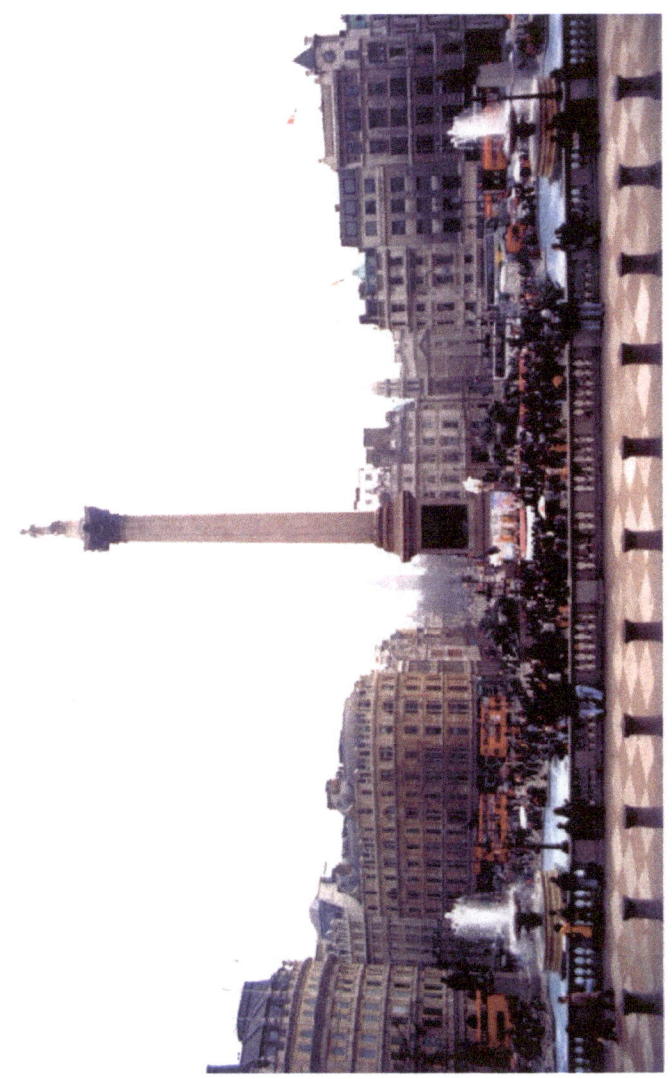

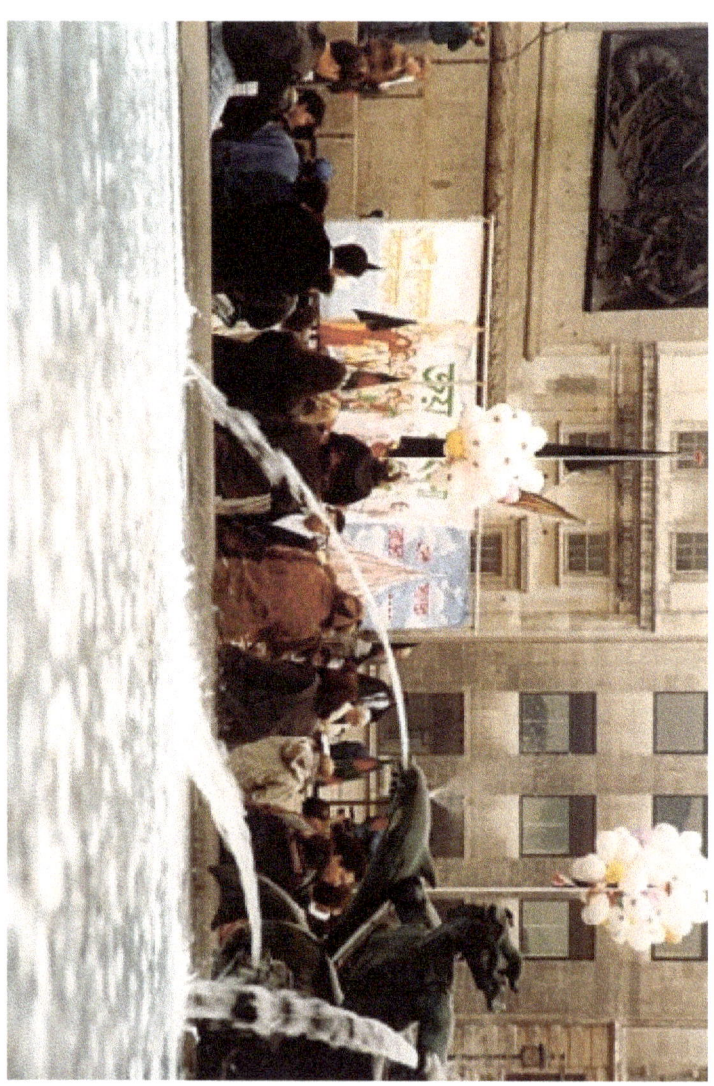

25th Anniversary of Bangladesh in Trafalgar Squares

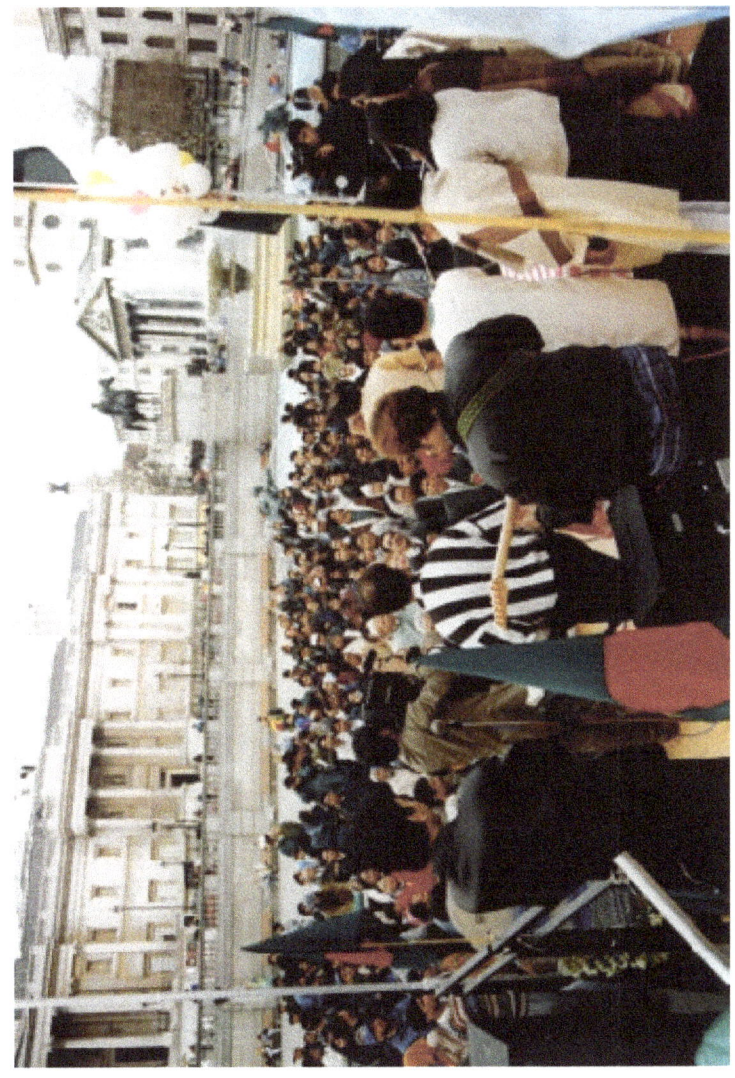

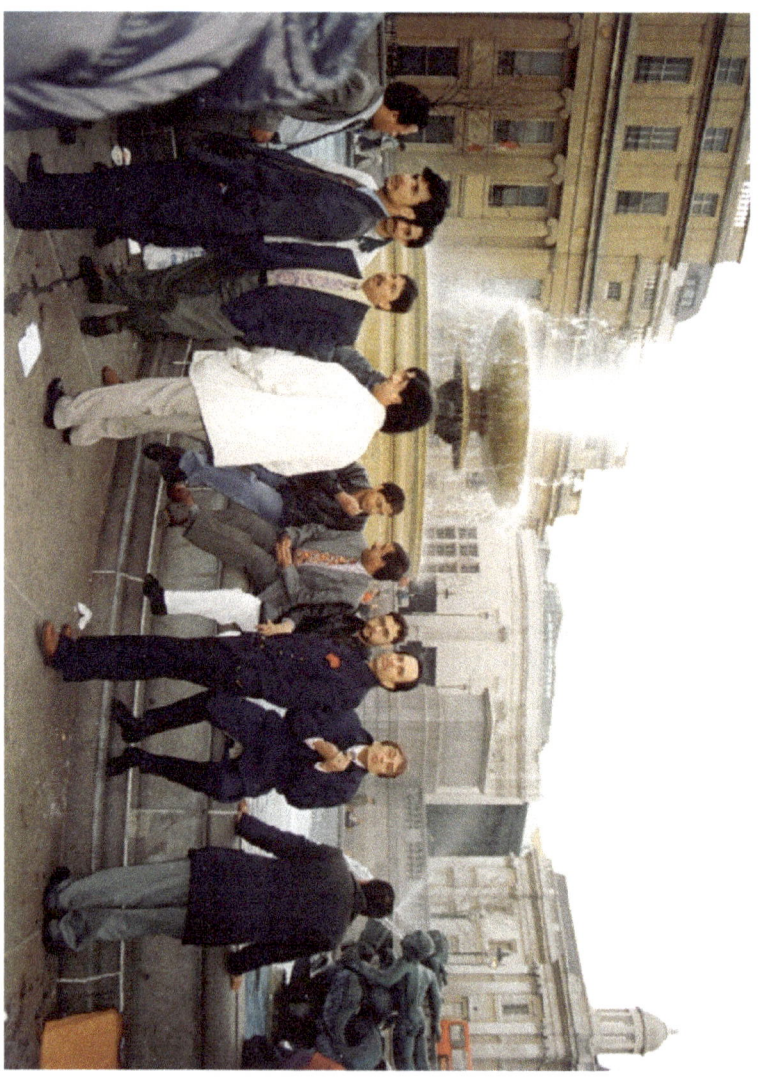

25th Anniversary of Bangladesh in Trafalgar Squares

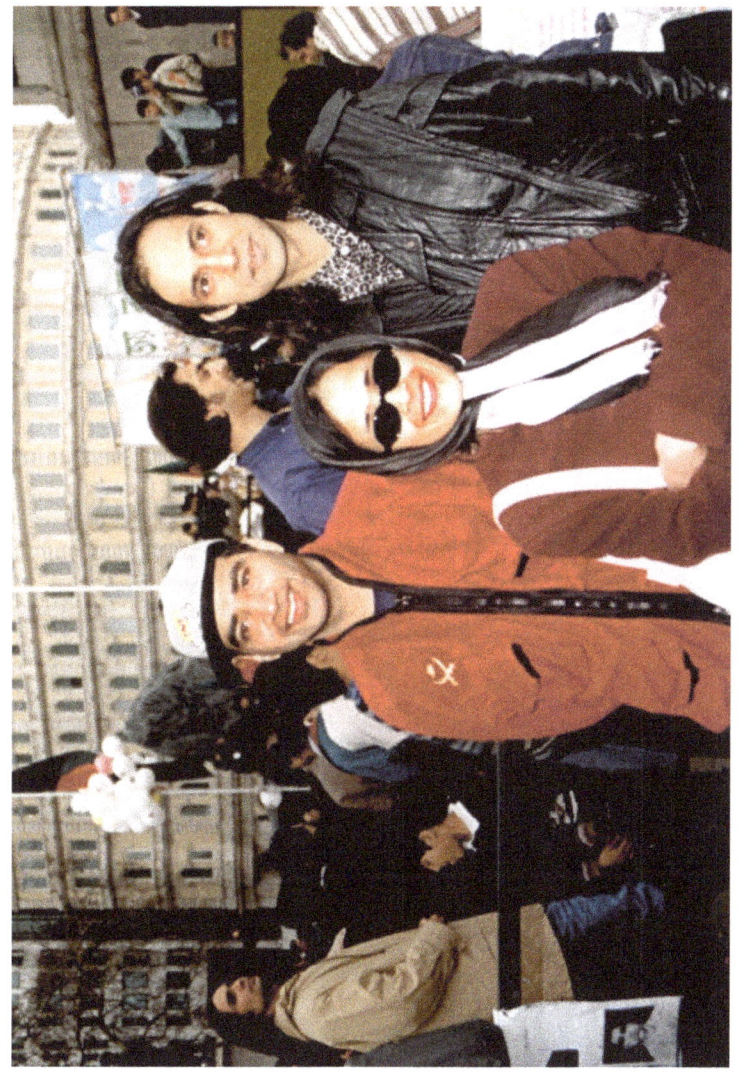

Nearer to the end, there was stall Islamic group.

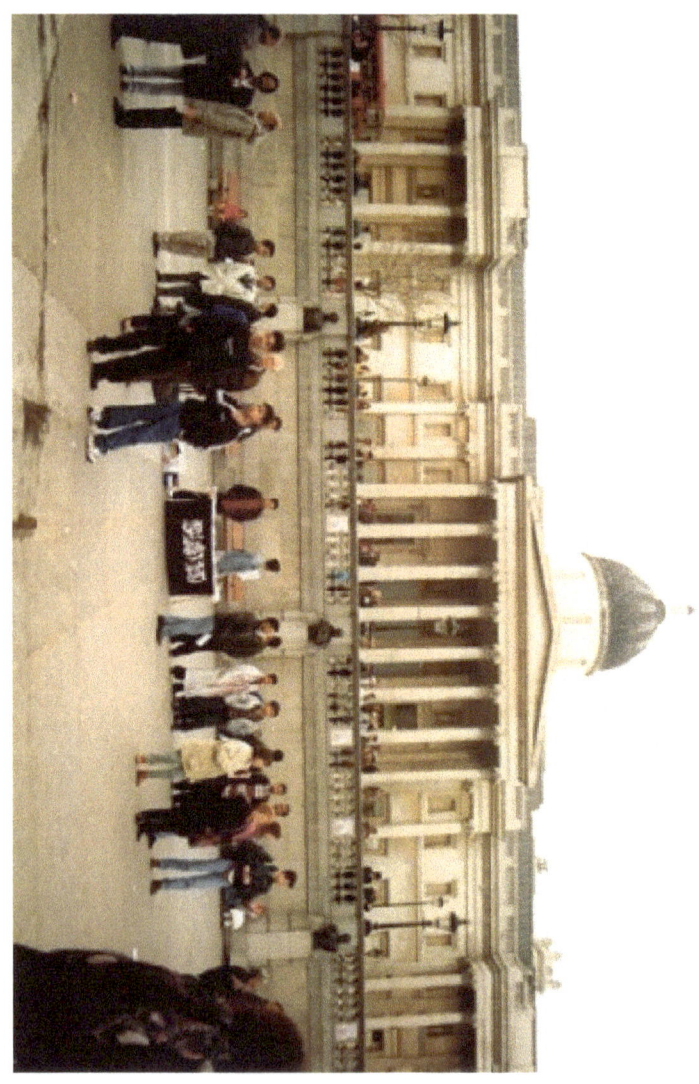

Joy Bangla

Joy Bangla!
Our sonar Bangladesh
Victorious souls
That ripples the nation

Joy Bangla!
Our land of joy and laughter
Home of our ancestors.

Joy Bangla!
Our mother land
Our fuel for hunger.

Joy Bangla!
Our sonar Bangla
Enriched with finest beauty.

A world of its own to be discovered.

The wisdom which lies untouched
Yet to be reborn
Yet to gain
And yet it shall rise again.

I wrote this poem when I was in school (1984-1989) Daneford Secondary Boys school, Bethnal Green, Tower Hamlets; as part of a cultural written event set by the then Head teacher, Mrs Chapman. Never written poems before.

I have also published this poem in my first poetry book in 2014, titled: "Father to Child,"

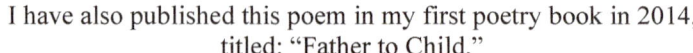

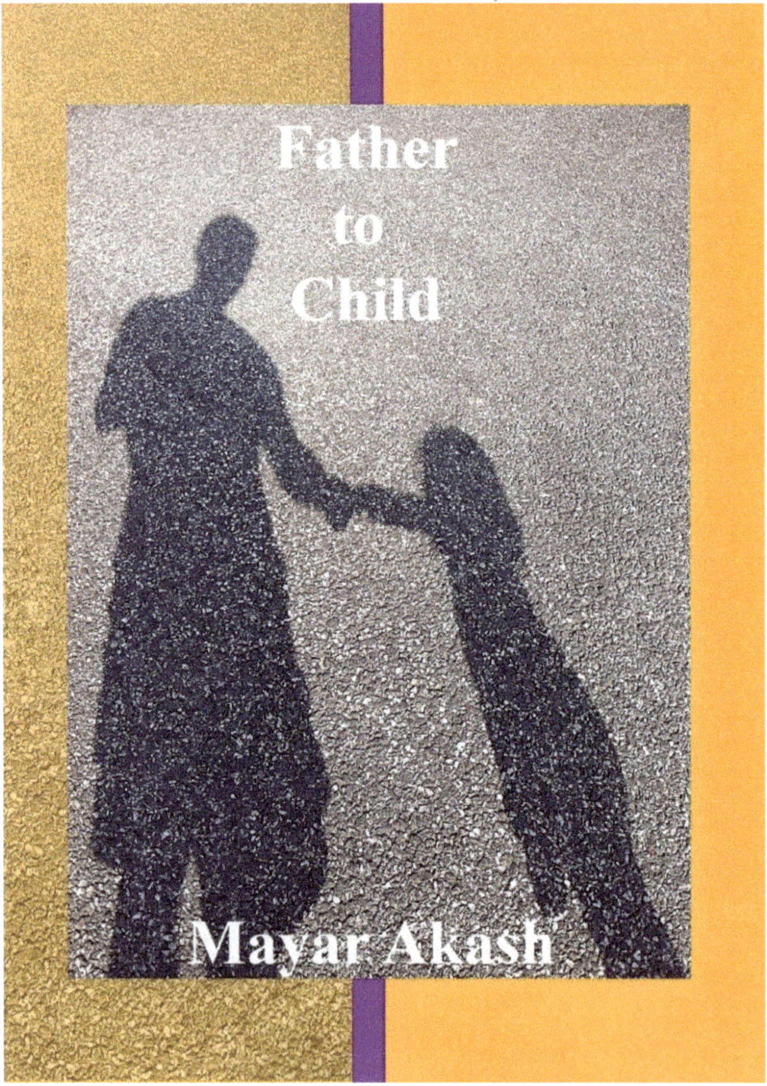

If you liked this book then you will like the others in the photo range.

25th Anniversary of Bangladesh in Trafalgar Squares

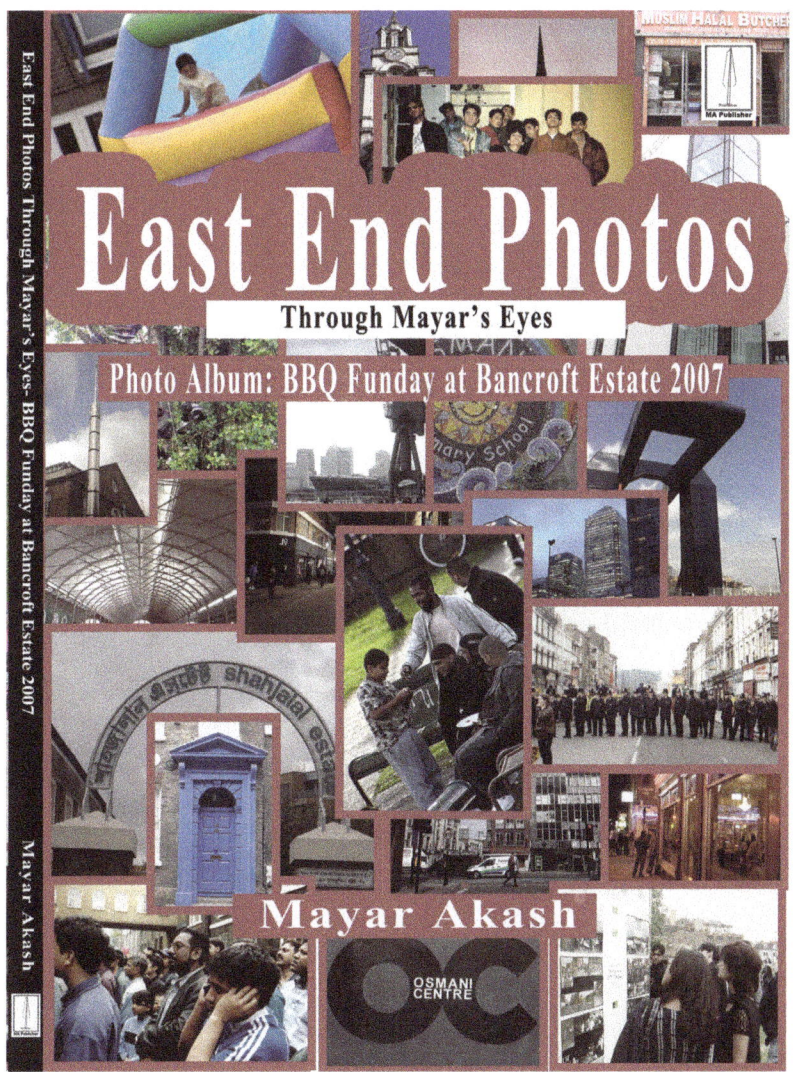

Photographs capturing the community coming together in Tower Hamlets in Bancroft Estate, E1.

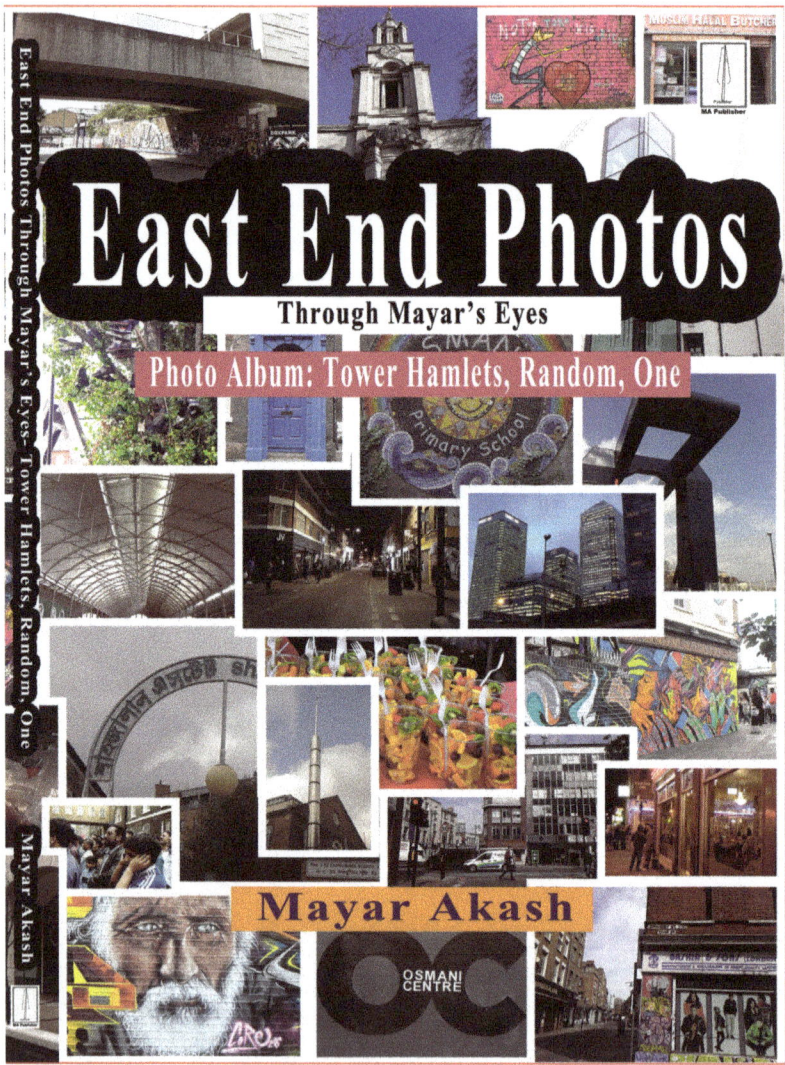

Photographs of Tower Hamlets, taken at random times, 1st collection.

25th Anniversary of Bangladesh in Trafalgar Squares

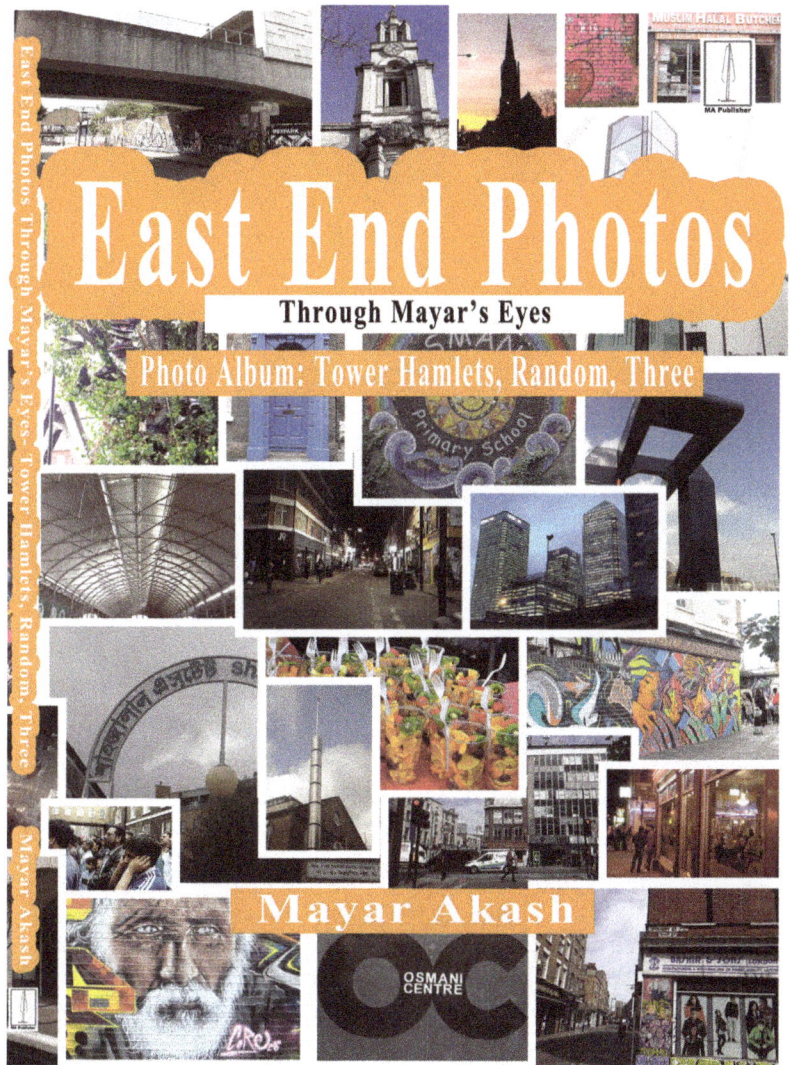

Photographs of Tower Hamlets, taken at random times, 3rd collection.

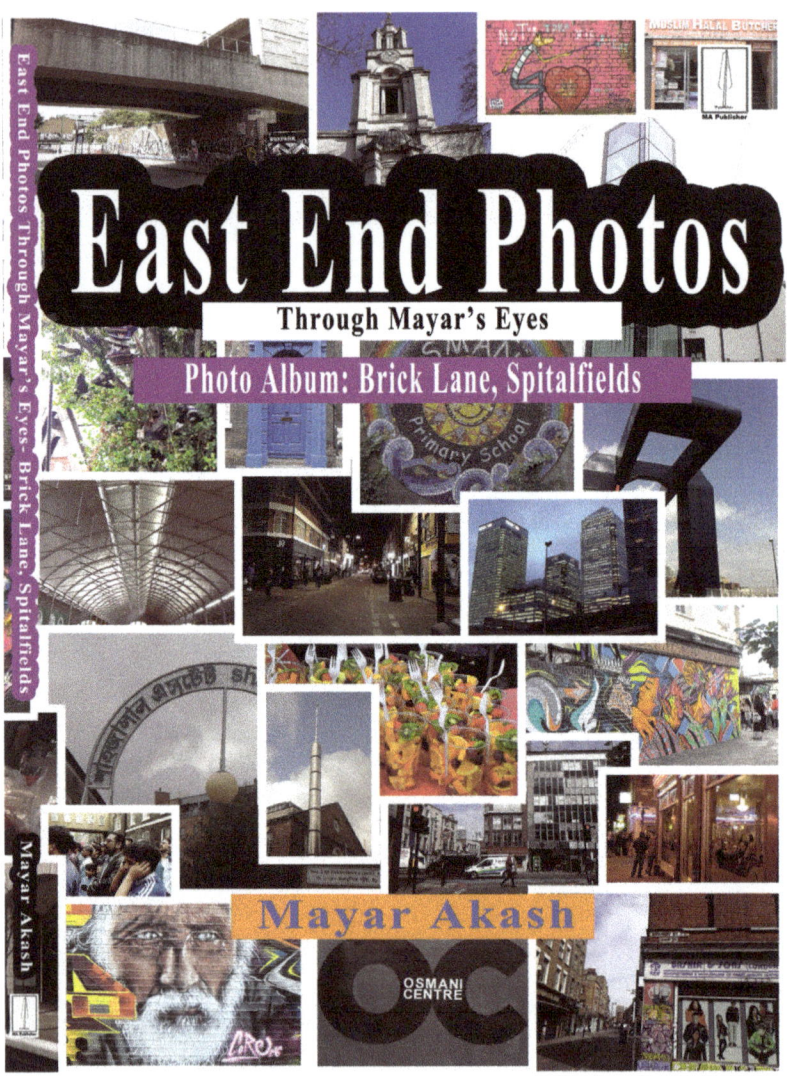

Photographs of Brick Lane, Spitalfields, Tower Hamlets.

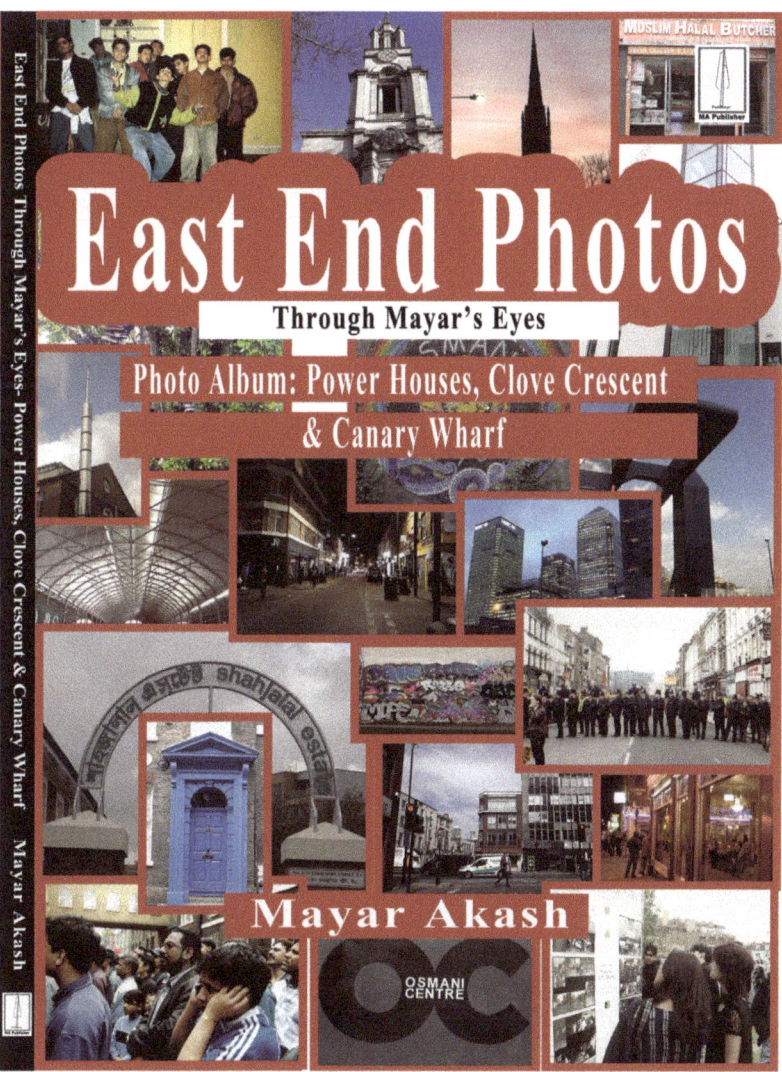

Photographs of Mulberry Place, Clove Crescent, Tower Hamlets, taken at random times.

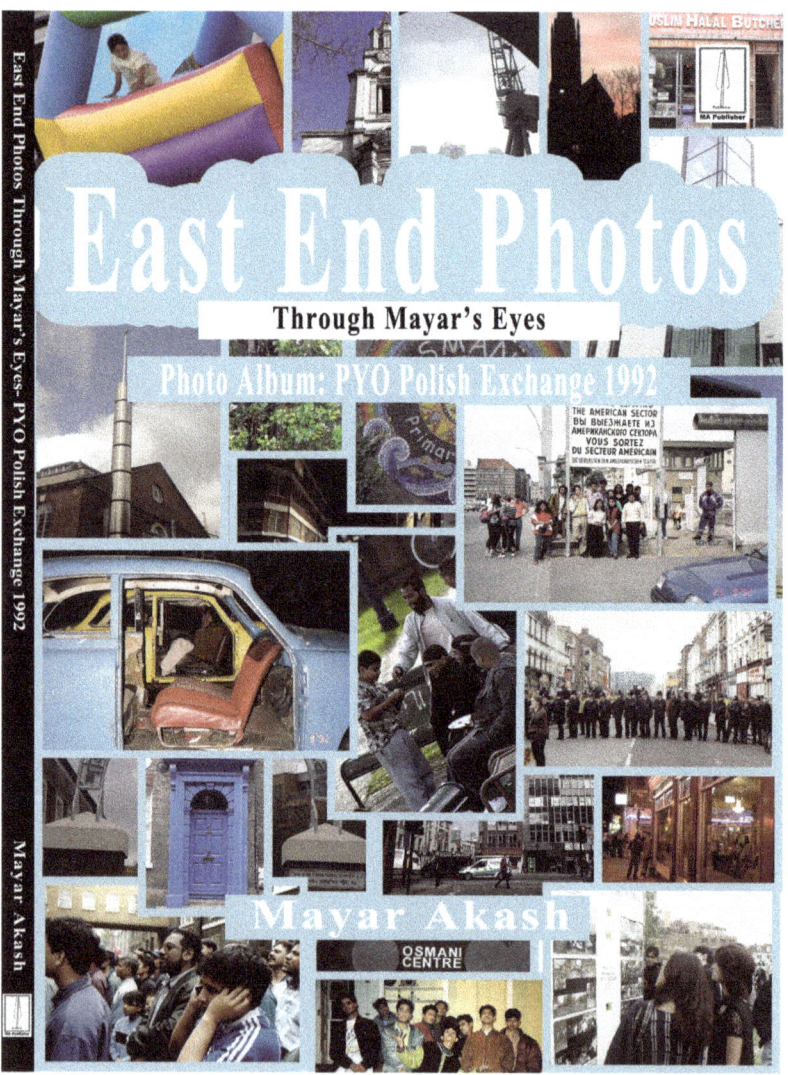

Photographs of Polish Exchange Trip by Progressive Youth Organisation (PYO) 1992

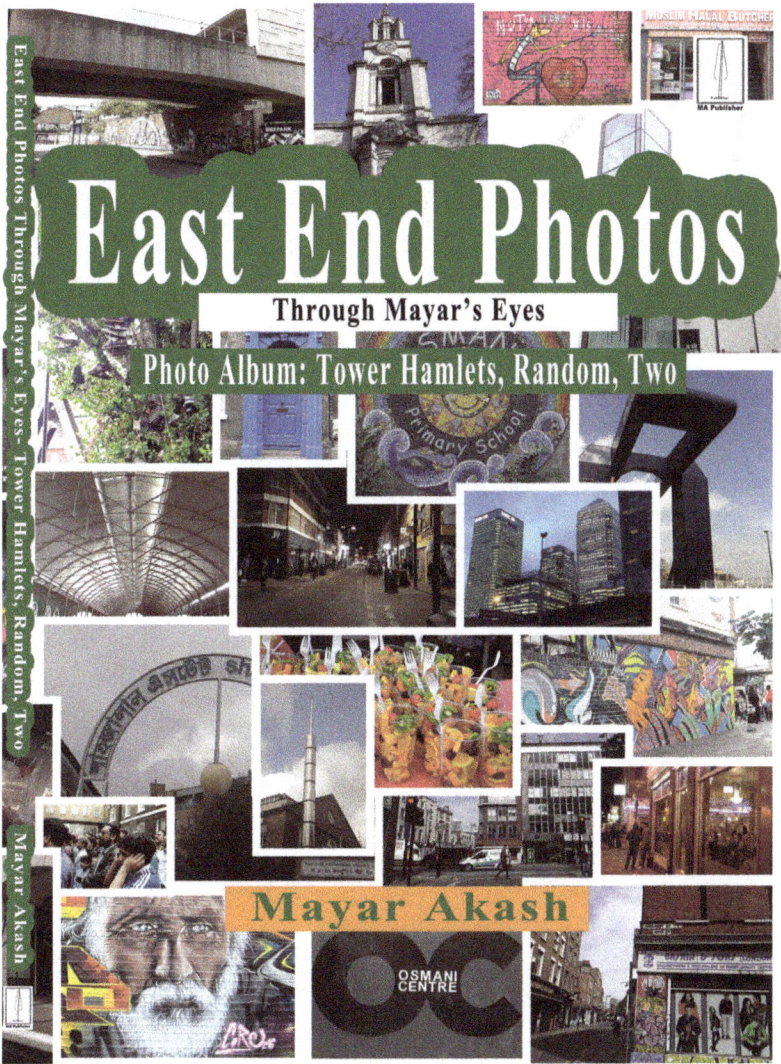

Photographs of Tower Hamlets, taken at random times, 2nd collection.

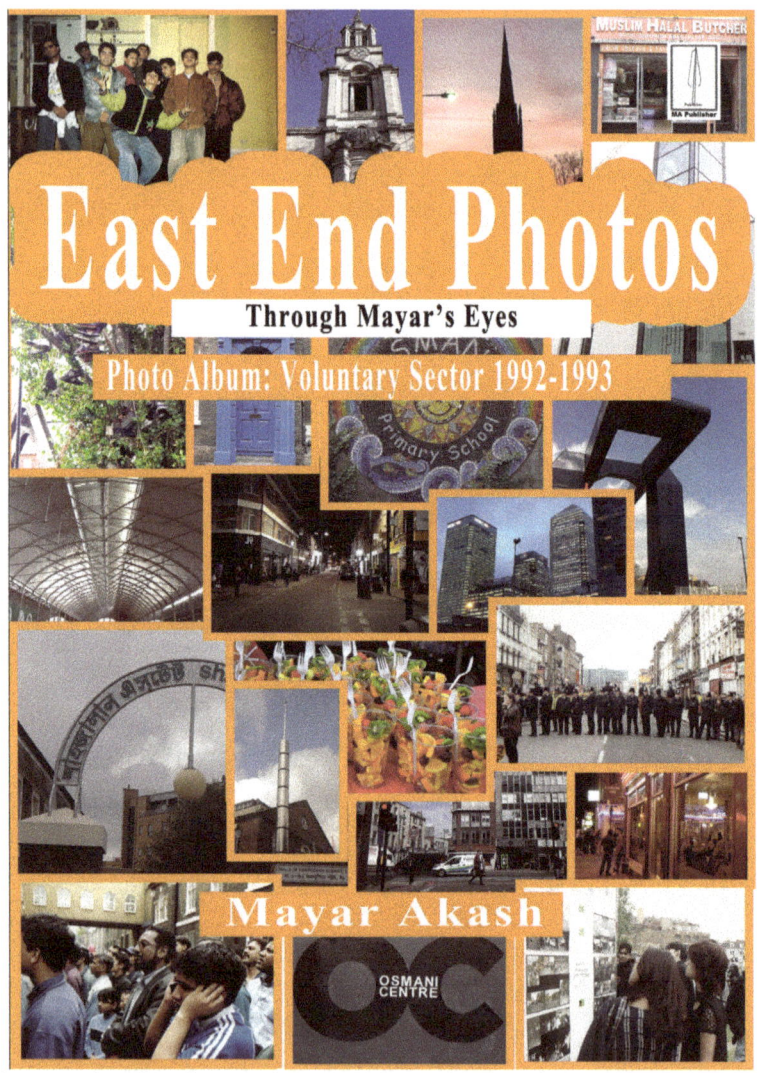

Photographs of Voluntary Sector, Progressive Youth Organisation (PYO) 1992-1993, Tower Hamlets.

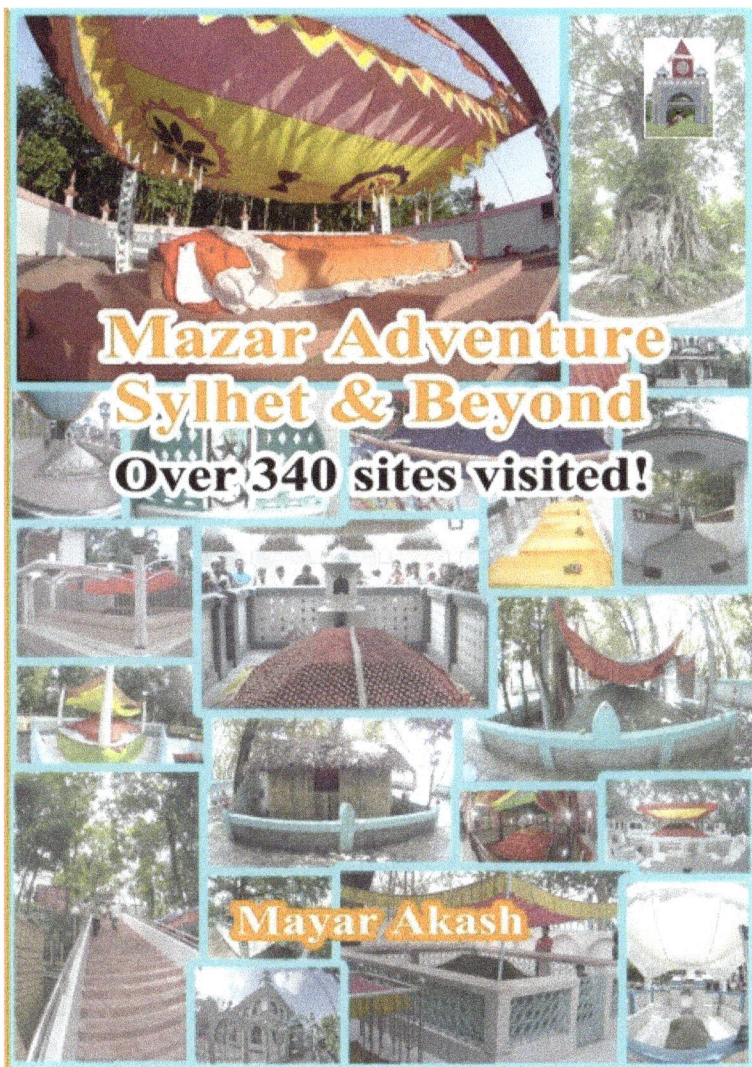

Photographs of Mazaar, Shrines, Mausoleums of Sylhet & Dhaka, Bangladesh

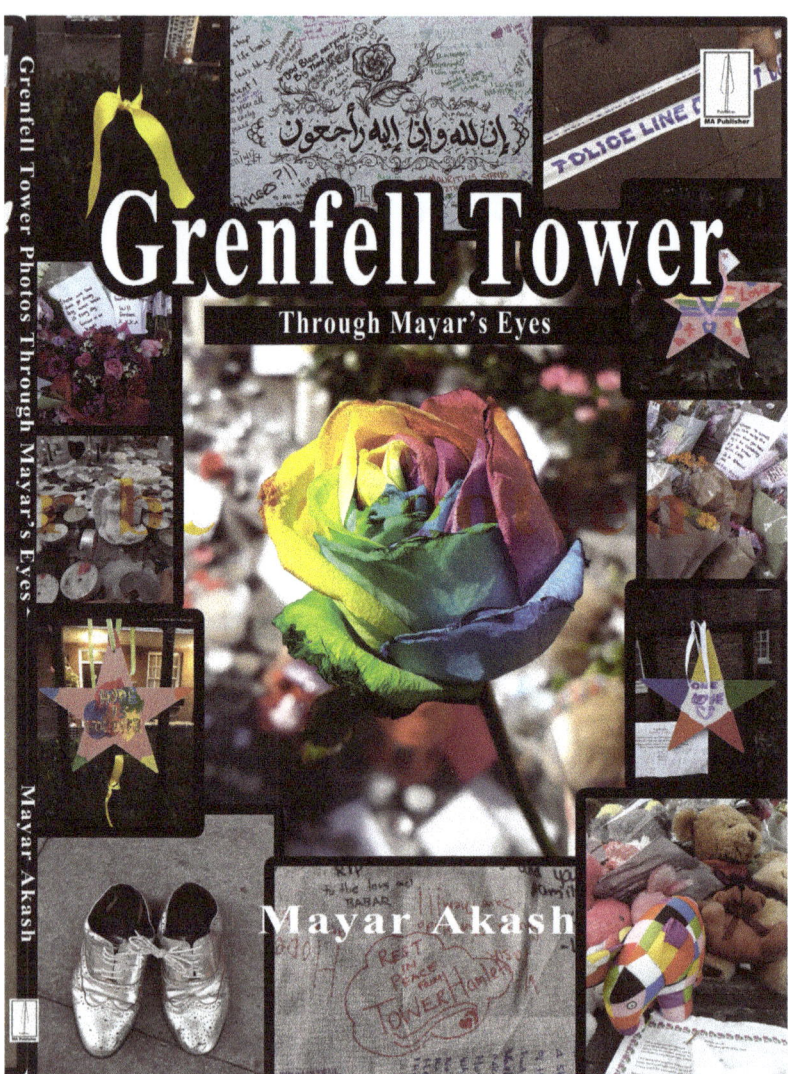

Photographs of the tragedy and the acknowledgements of the dead

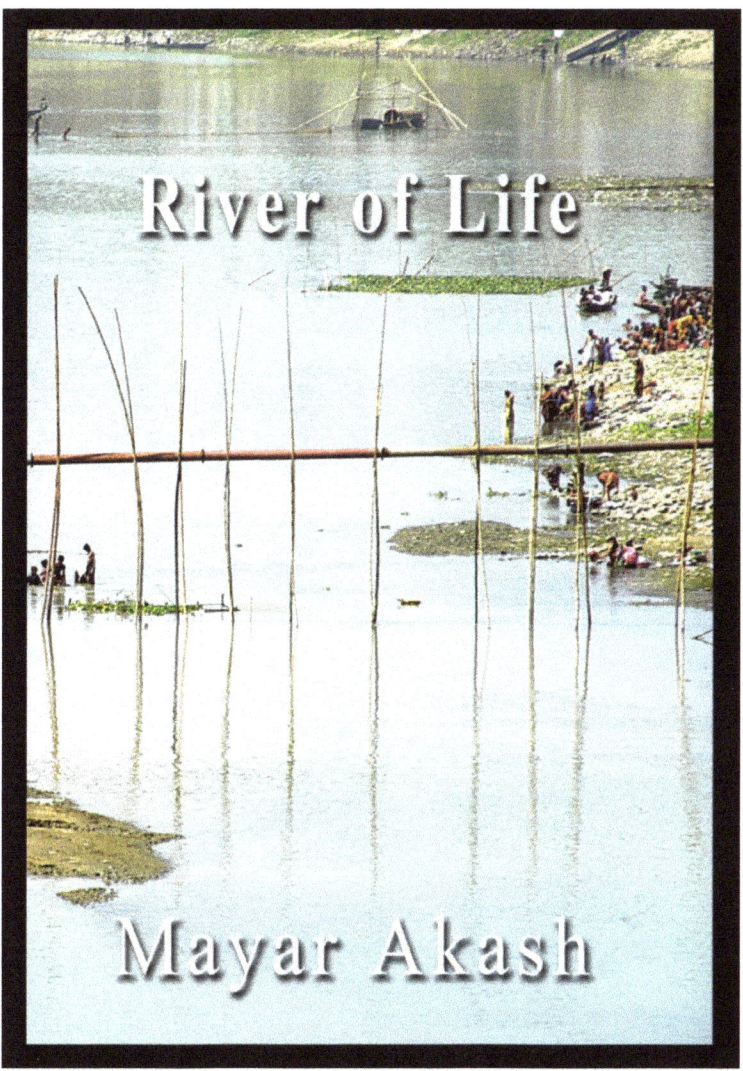

Autobiography – My journey down the River of Live

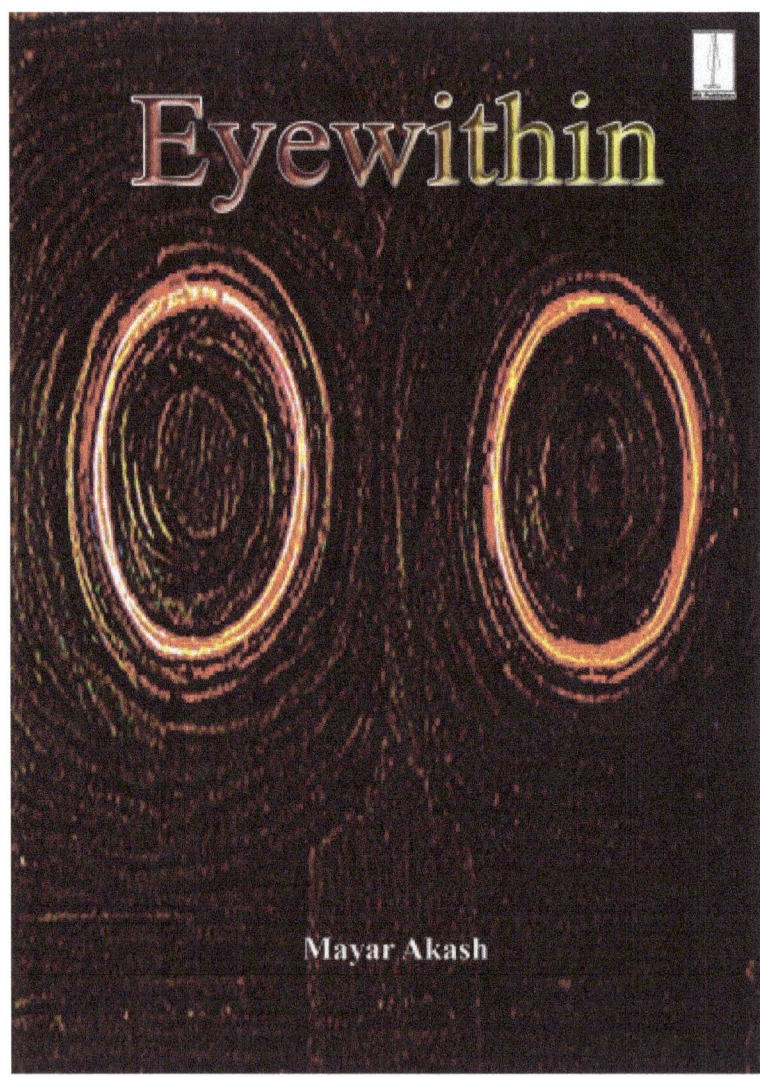

Autobiography through my artwork

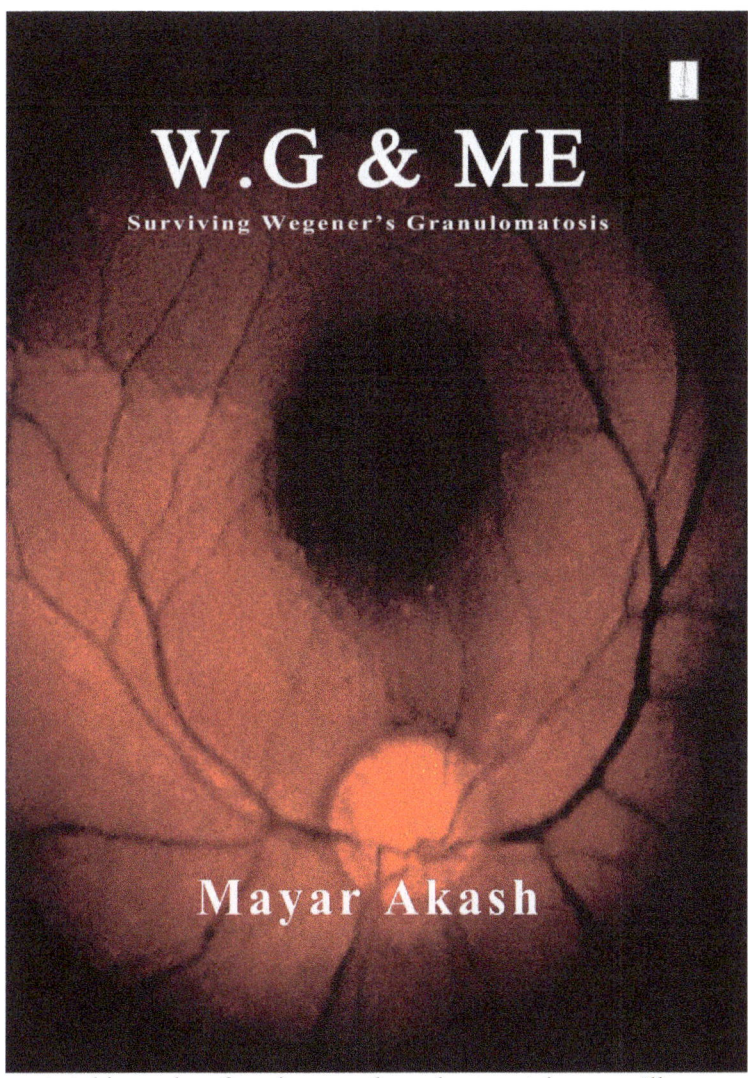

Autobiography of my journey through my autoimmune Illness

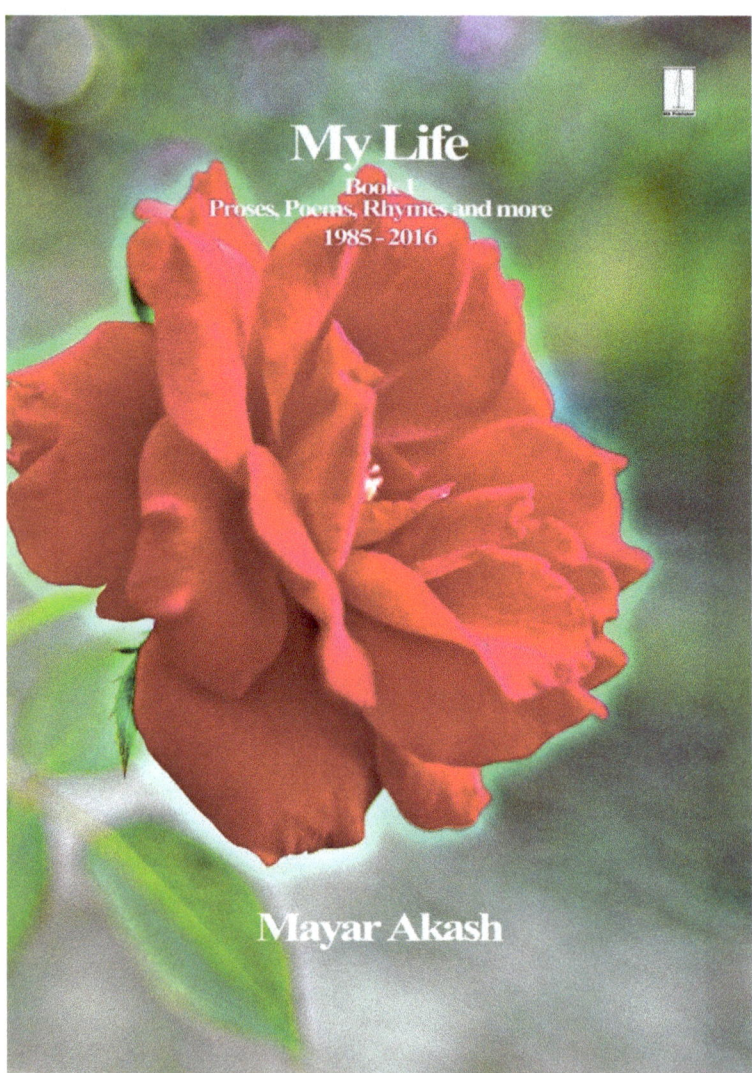

My poetry collection 1

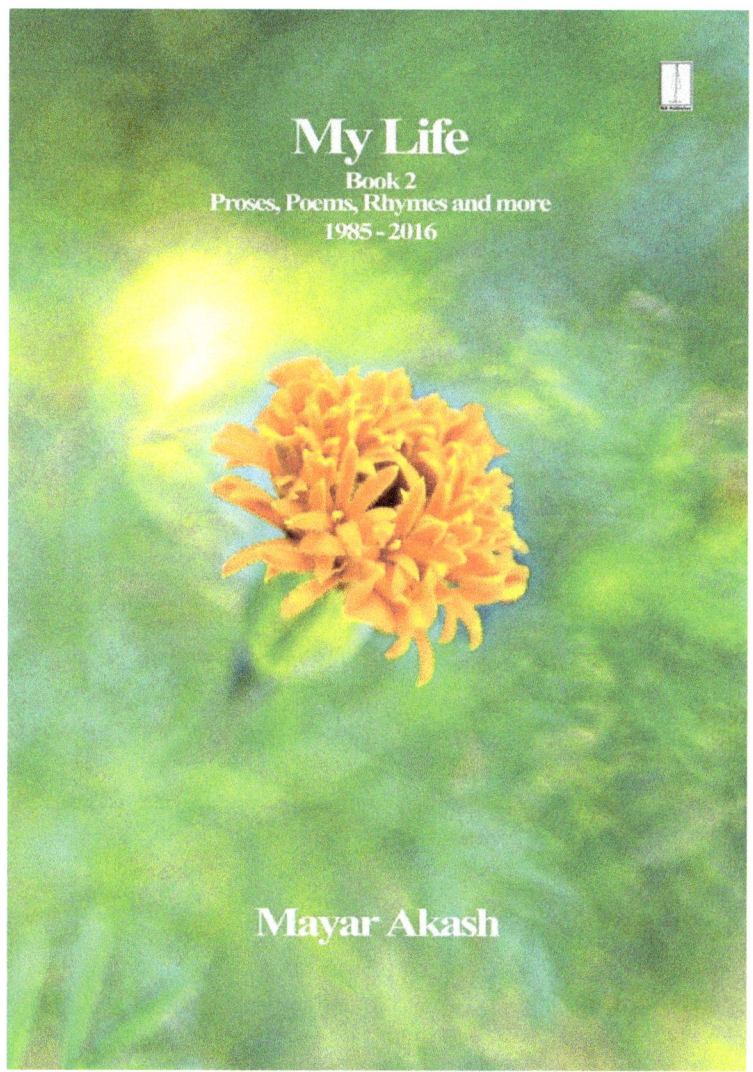

My poetry collection 2

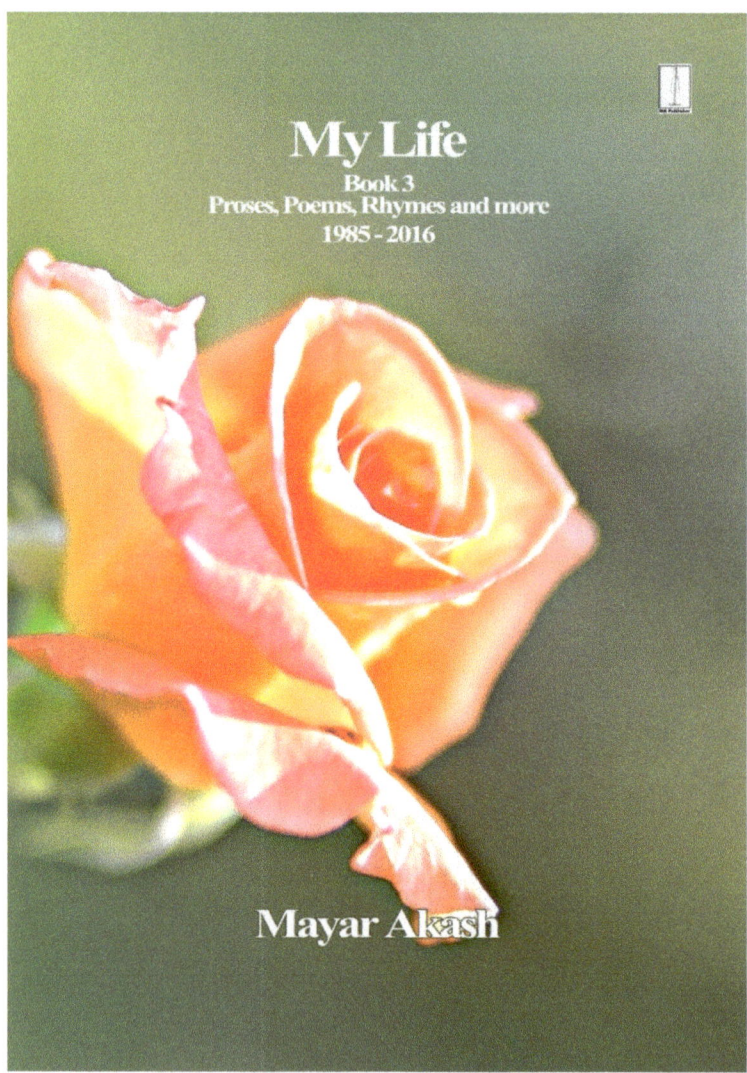

My poetry collection 3

25th Anniversary of Bangladesh in Trafalgar Squares

MAPublisher Catalogue

ISBN/Titles /Image/Author	ISBN/Titles /Image/Author	ISBN/Titles /Image/Author	ISBN/Titles /Image/Author
978-1-910499-00-9 Father to child By Mayar Akash	978-1-910499-08-5 HSJ Lakri Tura By Mayar Akash	978-1-910499-26-9 Colouring 1-10 By MAPublisher	978-1-910499-18-4 Basic Numbers 1-10 By MAPublisher
978-1-910499-16-0 River of Life By Mayar Akash	978-1-910499-09-2 HSJ Gilaf Procession By Mayar Akash	978-1-910499-27-6 Activity Numbers 1-10 By MAPublisher	978-1-910499-19-1 Number 1-100 By MAPublisher
978-1-910499-39-9 Eyewithin By Mayar Akash	978-1-910499-03-0 HSJ Mazar Sharif By Mayar Akash	978-1-910499-28-3 Activity Colouring Alphabets By MAPublisher	978-1-910499-20-7 Vowels By MAPublisher
978-1-910499-32-0 WG Survivor By Mayar Akash	978-1-910499-06-1 Hazrat Shahjalal By Mayar Akash	978-1-910499-68-9 The Adventures of Sylheti mazars By Mayar Akash	978-1-910499-21-4 Alphabet Consonants By MAPublisher
978-1-910499-66-5 Yesteryears By Mayar Akash	978-1-910499-07-8 HSJ Urus By Mayar Akash	978-1-910499-38-2 Bite Size Islam: 99 Names of Allah By Mayar Akash	978-1-910499-22-1 Vowels & Short By MAPublisher

121

ISBN/Titles /Image/Author	ISBN/Titles /Image/Author	ISBN/Titles /Image/Author	ISBN/Titles /Image/Author
978-1-910499-15-3 Anthology One By Penny Authors	978-1-910499-36-8 Delirious By Liam Newton	978-1-910499-52-8 Lit From Within By Ruth Lewarne	978-1-910499-57-3 The Vampire of the Resistance By Ruth Lewarne
978-1-910499-17-7 Anthology Two By Penny Authors	978-1-910499-54-2 Book of Lived v6 Penny Authors	978-1-910499-49-8 Cry for Help By B. M. Gandhi	978-1-910499-55-9 Riversolde By Meriyon
978-1-910499-29-0 Book of Lived v3 By Penny Authors	978-1-910499-37-5 When You Look Back By Rashma Mehta	978-1-910499-14-6 The Halloweeen Poem by Zainab Khan	978-1-910499-70-2 Smiley & The Acorn By Roger Underwood
978-1-910499-351 V4 Book of Lived By Penny Authors	978-1-910499-37-5 My Dream World By Rashma Mehta	978-1-910499-69-6 Consciousness By Mustak Mustafa	978-1-910499-40-5 World's First University By Giasuddin Ahmed
978-1-910499-50-4 Book of Lived v5 By Penny Authors	978-1-910499-53-5 Angel Eyez By Rashma Mehta	978-1-910499-73-3 Book of Lived v7 By Penny Authors	978-1-910499-56-6 The Warrior Queen By Giasuddin Ahmed

All books are available on-line, Google the titles and they will take you to the sites where you can acquire copies.

https://www.waterstones.com/author/mayar-akash/1973183 [3.11.21]

ISBN/Titles /Image/Author	ISBN/Titles /Image/Author	ISBN/Titles /Image/Author	ISBN/Titles /Image/Author
978-1-910499-58-0 Tower Hamlets, Random, One Mayar Akash	978-1-910499-60-3 Tower Hamlets, Random, Two By Mayar Akash	978-1-910499-05-4 Tide of Change By Mayar Akash	978-1-910499-51-1 Brick & Mortar By Mayar Akash
978-1-910499-61-0 Grenfell Tower By Mayar Akash	978-1-910499-63-4 Power Houses By Mayar Akash	978-1-910499-71-9 Altab Ali Murder By Mayar Akash	978-1-910499-31-3 Pathfinders By Mayar Akash
978-1-910499-62-7 Community Service 1992-1993 By Mayar Akash	978-1-910499-64-1 Bancroft Estate By Mayar Akash	978-1-910499-11-5 Re-Awakening By Mayar Akash	978-1-910499-13-9 Chronicle of Sylhetis of UK By Mayar Akash
978-1-910499-59-7 Brick Lane, Spitalfields By Mayar Akash	978-1-910499-72-6 25th Anniversary of Bangladesh By Mayar Akash	978-1-910499-12-2 Young Voice Mayar Akash	978-1-910499-42-9 Bangladeshi Fishes By Mayar Akash
978-1-910499-65-8 PYO Polish Exchange 1992 By Mayar Akash	978-1-910499-30-6 TH Bangladeshi Politicians By Mayar Akash	978-1-910499-10-8 Vigil Subotaged By Mayar Akash	978-1-910499-67-2 F. Ahmed and History By Mukid Choudhury

All books are available on-line, Google the titles and they will take you to the sites where you can acquire copies.
https://www.lulu.com/spotlight/mayarakash3bb00494 [10.11.21]

ISBN/Titles /Image/Author	ISBN/Titles /Image/Author	ISBN/Titles /Image/Author	ISBN/Titles /Image/Author
978-1-910499-43-6 My Life Book 1 By Mayar Akash	978-1-910499-44-3 My Life Book 2 By Mayar Akash	978-1-910499-45-0 My Life Book 3 By Mayar Akash	978-1-910499-46-7 My Life Book 4 By Mayar Akash
978-1-910499-47-4 My Life Book 5 By Mayar Akash	978-1-910499-75-7 Bangladeshis in Manchester - Oral History, Part 1 By M.A. Mustak	978-1-910499-74-0 Peter Fox Artist (LE) By Peter Fox	978-1-910499-76-4 Peter Fox Artist (POD) By Peter Fox
978-1-910499-78-8 On The Seventh Day By Cosette Ratliff	978-1-910499-77-1 Treasure on the Isles of Scilly By Roger Underwood		

All books are available on-line, Google the titles and they will take you to the sites where you can acquire copies.

You will also find the on-line catalogue on the following link.
https://www.lulu.com/spotlight/mayarakash3bb00494 [11.02.22]

These books are available on-line through Lulu.com and Amazon. They are also available in the book shop through their ISBN numbers.

www.ingramcontent.com/pod-product-compliance
Lightning Source LLC
Chambersburg PA
CBHW040517220526
45473CB00012B/2889